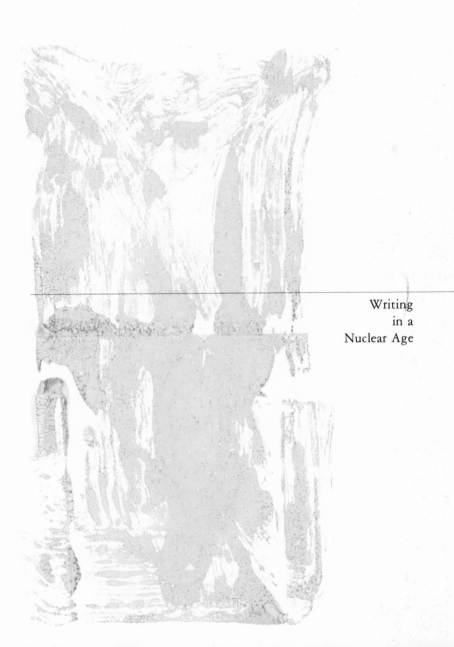

Writing
in a
Nuclear Age

Writing in a Nuclear Age

edited by
Jim Schley

New England Review
and
Bread Loaf Quarterly

distributed by
University Press of New England
Hanover
and London

Distributed by University Press of New England, Hanover, NH 03755
Printed in the United States by Northlight Studio Press, Barre, Vermont
Book design by Kate Emlen
Cover photo by Skip Schiel. The masks pictured were made for the play *FIRE* by Peter Schumann's Bread and Puppet Theater.

The first edition of this collection comprised Volume V, number 4 (Summer, 1983) of *NER / BLQ: New England Review and Bread Loaf Quarterly*. We are grateful to the following for permission to include material in this second edition:

"If On Account of the Political Situation," copyright © 1972 by W.H. Auden. Reprinted from W.H. AUDEN: COLLECTED POEMS, edited by Edward Mendelson, by permission of Random House, Inc.
"Wronke, Spring 1917" from "Threads: Rosa Luxemburg from Prison," copyright © 1978 by Jane Cooper. Quotes from Luxemburg's PRISON LETTERS TO SOPHIE LIEBKNECHT are courtesy of Independent Labour Publications, Leeds, England.
"Credo" by Michael Daley appears in his book THE STRAITS (Empty Bowl), copyright © by Michael Daley 1983.
"Self / Landscape / Grid" copyright © 1983 by Terrence Des Pres.
"Ground Zero" by Sharon Doubiago first appeared in *The Dalmo'ma Anthology*, (Empty Bowl).
"The Reading Club" reprinted by permission, copyright © 1983 by Patricia Goedicke. Originally in *The New Yorker*.

"The Birthplace" previously appeared in the *London Review of Books*, and will be part of Seamus Heaney's new collection, STATION ISLAND, to be published by Farrar, Straus, and Giroux, Inc. in December, 1984.
"The Fundamental Project of Technology" reprinted by permission. Copyright © 1984 by Galway Kinnell.
"After Labor Day" reprinted by permission, copyright © 1983 by Sydney Lea. Originally in *The New Yorker*.
"Spuyten Duyvil" originally appeared in *The Village Voice*, June 15, 1982. Copyright © 1982 by Honor Moore.
"Einstein's Bathrobe" has appeared in RULES OF SLEEP, copyright © 1984 by Howard Moss. Reprinted by permission of Atheneum, Inc.
"Return by Water" first appeared in *Ironwood*, copyright © 1984 by Jim Schley. Reprinted by permission of Michael Cuddihy.
"New Dawn" will appear in NEW AND SELECTED POEMS, 1923-1985, by Robert Penn Warren. Copyright © 1983 by Robert Penn Warren. Reprinted by permission of Random House, Inc.

Library of Congress Cataloging in Publication Data
Main entry under title:

Writing in a nuclear age.

Reprint of a special issue (summer 1983) of New England review and Bread Loaf quarterly with title: Writers in the nuclear age.
    1. Nuclear disarmament—Literary collections.
2. Antinuclear movement—Literary collections.
3. Nuclear warfare and society—Literary collections.
4. American literature—20th century. I. Schley, Jim, 1956-   . II. Writers in the nuclear age.
PS509.A85W74   1984   810'.8'00358   84-22666
ISBN 0-87451-319-7

Contents

Resolves

Preface

Two and a half years ago, when this collection began to take shape, I realized my motives as editor were personal as well as public. Like many others, I had been troubled by a split between my political activities and my work as a poet. Some days, this schism was not only frustrating but painful. Why was it so easy to write a letter-to-the-editor filled with opinions about disarmament, the war in Central America, or U.S. investment in South Africa, yet so difficult to write a poem that adequately reflected my concern for these matters? Having learned a great deal from the activist groups of which I have been a part, I hoped that a group of writers would be willing to address not just the subject of nuclear danger, but the nature of our awareness of that danger, our insights and evasions, and the *forms* of our responses. It seemed that by scrutinizing the ways expressive poets and fiction writers approach the theme of planetary annihilation, we would reveal much about the ways people are thinking and feeling right now.

We live in a world impoverished by preparations for the ultimate war. While claims and threats made in the name of "defense" by various leaders have grown ever more grandiose, there is epidemic hunger, infant mortality, illiteracy, and unemployment. More and more apparent is an epidemic anxiety: people everywhere are terrified of the carnage that would result from detonation of even one of the fifty thousand or more nuclear weapons presently stockpiled. Psychologists, social workers, and philosophers are telling us that anticipation of a nuclear catastrophe has immeasurably affected human perceptions, even in very small children.

Meanwhile, there is a countervailing wave. I know I am lucky to have lived in New England for almost ten years, where we've seen the evolution of a very large, visible, and affirmative peace movement; where issues such as war tax resistance, foreign intervention, and economic and environmental well-being are vigorously discussed in town assemblies, in the daily newspapers, and at a continuous round of meetings among citizens. This has been true in other parts of the country, as well. Physicians, teachers, parents, veterans, and others have gathered to consider what can be done to contend with the fear now evident in almost everyone. In a similar way, imaginative writers have taken up an often fierce debate about the relationships between politics and the literary arts. I am reminded of Moneta's challenge to Keats's "half-rotted" poet:

> What benefit canst thou do, or all thy tribe,
> To the great world? Thou art a dreaming thing,
> A fever of thyself— think of the earth

The works assembled here represent an increasingly widespread response, for contemporary writers hear that same challenge— internally, and also directly from readers and listeners. As crucial as the many books of analysis, statistics, history, and documentation have been to our understanding of the arms race and its effects, people seem to be craving more, in different forms. The first edition of this anthology was sold out in six months, suggesting perhaps that readers find poetry and fiction particularly eloquent in dramatizing certain immediate, visceral conditions of their lives.

Those works which reveal something new, or which most effectively challenge and console, may not depict the Bomb explicitly, but perhaps render by implication that sensation so common to our time: a ripping sound inside, a shadow that falls on some daily experience, as we weed the tomatoes, ride to work, or tie a child's shoelaces. This kind of portrayal is not only more complex than bare rhetoric in terms of craft, but also truer to the ways human feelings move. Our apprehension is usually not analytical, but instinctive and momentary. What artists can translate with special veracity and compassion are the repercussions of those instances of intru-

sion, mortification, and awe— which occur all the time—
when sirens switch on or a plane rumbles in low over the
houses and treetops. Psychologist Robert Jay Lifton has said
that at these moments nuclear weapons are already being
used, repeatedly and simultaneously, exploding in millions of
heads. Hence, our particular, mutual, sickness at heart.

Yet just as the human race is the source of its own
greatest peril, we are now the only source of any hope. The
forty-seven men and women featured here use a multitude of
vocabularies, different means of grasping at truth. Some of
them have long been associated with social causes, but others
are experimenting with both subject and form, perhaps
assimilating the nuclear presence into their customary manner
of writing, or even drastically modifying the approach in the
service of some new conception of accuracy. Writing a
magnificent political story or poem is as difficult, but not
intrinsically more difficult, than writing a magnificent love
story or poem, with more similarity of risks and obstacles
than is usually acknowledged. In this anthology, the subject
is shared— a plausible, no longer metaphorical apocalypse—
and the emotional complexity of that subject requires a
striking range of stylistic and ethical strategies. Some of these
writers are circuitous, others direct. Some incorporate
technical data, quotations, or descriptions of the atom bomb-
ings of Japan. Some may even be said to be fascinated by the
problem, for its inherent revelations of human temperament
and history, while others grieve, openly and often angrily.
Still, this is not intended to be an ideological debate. No one
here claims to have the solution to the dilemma at hand.
Rather, these writers have tried to peer at our situation from
all kinds of angles, to see and speak in some cases from
perspectives not their own. The overall sequence of the book
has been devised as a journey, out of desperation and mourning toward determination for change.

My choices as editor have been personal, perhaps
idiosyncratic. I've made my judgments on the basis both of
thematic pertinence and literary merit, according to the ways
I understand either, in the hope of avoiding a merely
polemical atmosphere. Many other fiction writers and poets

are working in this vein, trying to redefine their relation to a society in serious trouble, and there have been several excellent magazine collections compiled, including *The Dalmo'ma Anthology: Literature and Commitment* (Empty Bowl, Port Townsend, Washington), *Art and Guns* (Poetry East, Charlottesville, Virginia), and *Warnings: An Anthology on the Nuclear Peril* (Northwest Review, Eugene, Oregon). The impact of these gatherings comes not only from the beauty and power of individual pieces, but also from the accumulating uproar. What all of these writers share is a devotion to language, and a sense of imperative: a willingness or compulsion to struggle with literature's bearing on survival. Theirs is a very basic consolation, that any effort to foster compassion and sustain alertness is brave, and necessary; that while no single act is enough, we are not, in fact, alone.

Our determination to prevent a war must be as intense as our dread of the nuclear blast. We need all of the moral clarity and political influence we can summon, and all of us must learn to resist, individually and together: to resist death, to resist pretenses of justice and security. Ours is a civilization at a decisive juncture. Here is a chorus for the time being, words from the lovers of words for life on this blue planet.

J.S.

Lyme, New Hampshire
September, 1984

W. H. Auden

If On Account of the Political Situation

If on account of the political situation,
There are quite a number of homes without roofs, and men,
Lying about in the countryside neither drunk nor asleep,
If all sailings have been cancelled till further notice,
If it's unwise now to say much in letters, and if,
Under the subnormal temperatures prevailing,
The two sexes are at the present the weak and the strong,
That is not at all unusual for this time of year.
If that were all, we should know how to manage. Flood, fire,
The destruction of grasslands, restraint of princes,
Piracy on the high seas, physical pain and fiscal grief,
These after all are our familiar tribulations,
And we have been through them all before, many, many, times.
As events which belong to the natural world where
The occupation of space is the real and final fact
And time turns round itself in an obedient circle,
They occur again and again but only to pass
Again and again into their formal opposites,
From sword to ploughshare, coffin to cradle, war to work,
So that, taking the bad with the good, the pattern composed
By the ten thousand odd things that can possibly happen
Is permanent in a general average way.

    Till lately we knew of no other, and between us we seemed
To have what it took — the adrenal courage of the tiger,
The chameleon's discretion, the modesty of the doe,
Or the fern's devotion to spatial necessity:
To practice one's peculiar civic virtue was not
So impossible after all; to cut our losses
And bury our dead was really quite easy: that was why
We were always able to say: we are the children of God,
And our father has never forsaken His people.

    But then we were children: that was a moment ago
Before an outrageous novelty had been introduced
Into our lives. Why were we never warned? Perhaps we were.
Perhaps that mysterious noise at the back of the brain

W.H. Auden

We noticed on certain occasions — sitting alone
In the waiting rooms of the country junction, looking
Up at the toilet window — was not indigestion
But this Horror starting already to scratch Its way in?
Just how, just when It succeeded we shall never know:
We can only say that now It is there and nothing
We learnt before It was there is now of the slightest use,
For nothing like It has happened before. It's as if
We had left our house for five minutes to mail a letter,
And during that time the living room had changed places
With the room behind the mirror over the fireplace;
It's as if, waking up with a start, we discovered
Ourselves stretched out flat on the floor, watching our shadow
Sleepily stretching itself at the window. I mean
That the world of space where events re-occur is still there
Only now, it's no longer real; the real one is nowhere
Where time never moves and nothing can ever happen:
I mean that although there's a person we know all about
Still bearing our name and loving himself as before,
That person has become a fiction; our true existence
Is decided by no one and has no importance to love.

That is why we despair; that is why we welcome
The nursery bogey or the winecellar ghost, why even
The violent howling of winter and war has become
Like a jukebox tune that we dare not stop. We are afraid
Of pain but more afraid of silence; for no nightmare
Of hostile objects could be as terrible as this void.
This is the abomination. This is the wrath of God.

Terrence Des Pres

Self / Landscape / Grid

Miller owns this field, Locke that, and Manning the woodland beyond. But none of them owns the landscape. There is a property in the horizon which no man has but he whose eye can integrate all the parts, that is, the poet.

— Emerson

Every appearance in nature corresponds to some state of mind....

— Emerson

I live in upstate New York, rural countryside and lovely hills, a place my neighbors like to call "the village." It's small, quiet, great for raising kids. Forty miles to the north, however, lies Griffiss Airforce Base, known locally as Rome, because Rome is the town the base uses. Out of there fly the B-52's that control our part of the sky. There too the Pentagon keeps its brood of cruise missiles. So nobody doubts, in this part of the country, that Rome (when it happens) will be the spot where the warheads hit. At one time we thought that the Russians had size but no technical finesse. That gave us a stupid sort of hope. An overshot might land on our heads, but if incoming missiles fell short, they would come down way north, maybe on Edmund Wilson's old stone house in Talcottville, and we, at least, would be well out of range. Now we are told that the Soviets have refined their delivery. Their guidance systems are on target, not least because the Russians have used American technology, computers, micro-chips, ball-bearings, made and sold by American firms. That, no matter how we look at it, is ugly news. And with Rome at the nub of a nuclear arc, we are resigned in our knowledge that things will start exactly forty miles away. How far the firestorm will reach is what we mainly wonder. We don't know, but we are counting on these upstate hills to block the worst of the blast. If the horizon works in our favor, we shall then have time to consider the wind. In the meantime, B-52's cross and recross above us. They gleam with their nuclear payload. Two or three are up there always, and once I counted thirteen. The air is creased with vapor trails, and in the afternoons, when the sun starts down, the sky looks welted with scars.

That, anyway, is the prospect I share with my neighbors, our part of the nuclear grid. Not a landscape of the mind, no inner weather sort of scene, it's just life's natural place for those who live here. Even so, the bombers overhead keep me reminded that this landscape possesses, or is possessed by, some other will, some demonic grand design or purpose not at all my own. Nor would that kind of death be mine. An all-at-once affair for almost everyone is how that death would come, impersonal but still no accident. That way of dying would be the ultimate instance of political intrusion, for that is what has brought us to this pass, politics, and by political intrusion I mean the increasing unsettlement and rending of our private lives by public force. We do what we can as citizens, but when it comes to nuclear war we can't do much. The hazard is before us and won't budge. How to live with it is our problem, and some of us, at least, resort to magic. We turn to words which give the spirit breathing space and strength to endure. As in any time of ultimate concern, we call on poetry.

I can read *Ecclesiastes* or *King Lear* for a language equal to extremity, but such language isn't of my time, not of my landscape perhaps I should say. I find a little of what I need in poets like Akhmatova or Mandelstam or Milosz, but American poetry? and among poets of the present generation? Not much, in fact hardly anything. I'm writing in early February (1983) and I've just gone through the recent issue of *American Poetry Review*, which offers forty-eight poems by twenty-one poets. Some few good poems, but only two touch upon our nuclear fate, which leaves forty-six in worlds elsewhere. In "Against Stuff" Marvin Bell follows the possibility—this is a night-thoughts poem—that all our forms and habits, including those of poetry itself, may have been wrong, wrong enough to bring us to "the coming instantaneous flaming" of all creatures and things "which could not suffer/that much light at one time." The poem spreads disquiet and resists reply, and in the following lines the pun on "not right" keeps the poet honestly uncertain:

> and, if we are shortly to find ourselves
> without beast, field or flower,

is it not right that we now prepare
by removing them from our poetry?

Under nuclear pressure, should poetry contract its domain? The other poem in *APR*, Maxine Kumin's "You Are In Bear Country," moves with wit and nice inevitability to the imagined moment when the grizzly attacks—and then jumps to this question in italics:

> *Is death*
> *by bear to be preferred*
> *to death by bomb?*

The question seems to intrude out of nowhere, and the poet closes by answering yes. The point, I presume, is that any thought of death, even one so unlikely, recalls the nuclear alternative. And grotesque though it would be, death "by bear" does seem preferable, one's own at least, and natural, part of the order of things and an order, too, as timeless as the wilderness. Bizarre consolations, but once the nuclear element intrudes, these are the sorts of ludicrous lengths to which we feel pushed. And the either / or is not even a choice, but only a preference. The absence of *a* and *the* before *bear* and *bomb* suggests two categories of death, only one of which is humanly acceptable.

After *APR* I went on to *Poetry,* where there was nothing relevant, and after that I rummaged randomly through the library's stock of recent journals and magazines, all I could manage in two afternoons. I am sure I read more than two hundred poems, most of them quite short, some very good, but none informed by nuclear awareness. I realize, of course, that any successful poem must authorize itself, must utter its world with self-certainty, but even so, reading so many poems one after the other left me rather shocked by the completeness, the sealed-up way these poems deny the knowledge or nearness of nuclear threat. The other striking thing about most of these poems was their sameness, and especially the meagreness. These observations are not original, of course. Lots of poetry gets written and published in American just now, and if one reads even a small but steady portion of it, one starts to see that the current talk about a "crisis" in our poetry is not unfounded. The trivialization, the huddled stance, the seemingly deliberate littleness of so much poetry in the last few years—how shall we account for it?

Perhaps the rise of the "work-shop" poem has had something to do with it. Maybe also the new careerism among younger poets bent on bureaucratic power in the universities; those who, as Marx would say, have gone over to the management. And surely the kind of literary criticism now in vogue, hostile to the integrity of language, doesn't help. But these are as much symptoms as causes, and the larger situation comes down to this: In a time of nuclear threat, with absolutely everything at stake, our poetry grows increasingly claustrophilic and small-themed, it contracts its domain, it retires still further into the narrow chamber of the self; and we see in this not only the exhaustion of a mode and a tradition, but also the spectacle of spirit cowed and retreating.

The retreat has been swift because American practice invites it. Founded on Emersonian principles, our poetry has drawn much of its strength from an almost exclusive attention to self and nature. Typically we have conceived of the self *as* a world rather than of the self *in* the world. Things beyond the self either yield to imagination or else they don't matter, and the world becomes a store of metaphor to be raided as one can. The "strong" poet turns any landscape to private use, and solipsism wins praise as the sign of success. Emerson didn't invent these attitudes, but he was good at summing them up. "Every natural fact is a symbol of some spiritual fact," he wrote, and "the Universe is the externization [sic] of the soul." Thus the road was open for Whitman and poets to come, and thus Emerson delivered his mandate: "Know then that the world exists for you," and "Build therefore your own world." Partly, this is the mythology of our national experience, with its determination to deny social-political limits and focus instead on individual destiny. Partly, too, this is the American brand of Romanticism, part of a larger movement that on the continent peaked in its influential French example. Baudelaire called the world a "forest of symbols," and Mallarmé thought that everything external, *la cité, ses gouvernements, le code*, could be dismissed as *le mirage brutal*.

Stated thus, the whole business seems outlandish—but not really. The Emersonian mandate supports maximum belief in the poet's potency, not in itself a bad thing. Then, too, poets in our century have held some very odd convictions, Yeats for example, or for that matter, Merrill. But in one respect there is no doubting: American poetry has rejected history and politics on principle. Despite Lowell's example and more recent exceptions like Rich and Forché, our poets in the main have been satisfied to stick with Emerson, and few would find anything to take exception with in the following lines from Emerson's *Ode:*

> I cannot leave
> My honeyed thought
> For the priest's cant,
> Or statesman's rant.
>
> If I refuse
> My study for their politique,
> Which at the best is trick,
> The angry Muse
> Puts confusion in my brain.

American contempt for politicians runs deep. As a sort of common-sense cynicism it allows us to go untroubled by crime in high places and, more to the point, it bolsters our belief that personal life exists apart from, and is superior to, political force and its agencies. But also, as Gunnar Myrdal demonstrated in *An American Dilemma*, our sort of political cynicism goes hand in hand with a remarkably durable idealism. We take for granted that governments are corrupt, then feel that some other power, providential and beyond the meddling of men, governs our destiny finally. Where there's a will there's a way, and everything comes right in the end. But does it? Even without the Bomb to put such faith into question, Emerson's example — Poland, for God's sake! — invites scepticism:

> The Cossack eats Poland,
> Like stolen fruit;
> Her last noble is ruined,
> Her last poet mute:
> Straight, into double band
> The victors divide;
> Half for freedom strike and stand: —
> The astonished Muse finds thousands at her side.

The Muse might well be befuddled, given the logic of Emerson's syntax. But of course, Emerson's faith in the future—disaster compensated by renewal—can't mean much to us. With the advent of the nuclear age there is no assurance that anything will remain for the phoenix to rise from.

We have fallen from the Garden, and the Garden itself—nature conceived as an inviolate wilderness—is pocked with nuclear waste and toxic dumps, at the mercy of industry and Watt, all of it open to nuclear defilement. Generations come and go, but that *the earth abideth forever* is something we need to feel, one of the foundations of poetry and humanness, and now we are not sure. That is the problem with nuclear threat, simply as threat; it undermines all certainty, and things once absolute are now contingent. To feel that one's private life was in the hands of God, or Fate, or even History, allowed the self a margin of transcendence; the dignity of personal life was part of a great if mysterious Order. But now our lives are in the hands of a few men in the Pentagon and the Kremlin, men who, having affirmed that they would destroy us to save us, have certified their madness—and yet their will determines our lives and our deaths. We are, then, quite literally enslaved, and assuming that this bothers poets no less than the rest of us, why do they so seldom speak of it? It is not too much to say that most poetry in America is written against experience, against first feelings and needs. Whether the Emersonian tradition is a trap or a last-ditch defense is perhaps a moot point. But the poetry of self still predominates, with nature as its cornerstone, despite Los Alamos, a lovely spot in the mountains.

Nuclear wipe-out is possible, perhaps probable, and every day I talk with people who are convinced it will happen. No soul is free of that terror, nor of that knowledge; and simply as a state of mind or way of knowing, it drastically alters how we receive and value our experience. Birth, for example, or one's own death; surely having children troubles us in ways not known before, and we need to feel that each of us shall have a death of his or her own, simply in order to feel fully possessed of our lives. These are common feelings, and it's clearer than it used to be that no man (no, nor woman neither) is an island. Our surface lives are individual and unique, but human existence itself—the being that all of us share and feel threatened—gives us our most important sense of ourselves and, I should also think, gives poetry its most significant themes. Can it be, then, that the shallowness of recent poetry reveals a desperate clinging to the surface?

I do *not* ask for poems directly about the Bomb or the end of the world, although with the Bell poem in *APR* as evidence, a theme of this kind can be as legitimate as any other. I don't expect poems of protest or outrage or horror either, although again, I can't see that they would hurt. I do, however, try to keep in mind that some subjects are more human, and more humanly exigent than others—Forché on Salvador compared to Leithauser on dandelions—and also that poets are often scared off by subjects which, precisely because of the fear, signal a challenge worth the risk. But what I'd mainly hope to see, in this case, is poetry that probes the impact of nuclear threat, poetry informed by nuclear knowing, poems that issue from the vantage of a self that accepts its larger landscape, a poetic diction testing itself against the magnitude of our present plight, or finally just poems which survive their own awareness of the ways nuclear holocaust threatens not only humankind but the life of poetry itself.

Nature, for example, remains the mainstay of our poetry. Natural imagery makes us trust the poem, suggests a permanence at the root of things, and every poem about nature bears somewhere within it the myth of renewal and rebirth. But from the nuclear perspective, these ministrations falter. Permanence? Rebirth? Emerson's response to nature was genuinely poetic, and the measure of our present loss may be judged by the degree of nostalgia rather than assent we feel when he says: "In the woods, we return to reason and faith. There I feel that nothing can befall me in life,—no disgrace, no calamity (leaving me my eyes), which nature cannot repair." Well, his notion of calamity isn't ours. And nature, for all its proven renovative power, could never repair the worst that might befall us. Nature suffers the same division we observe in ourselves and in the landscape generally. We are what we are, yet some deep part of selfhood has been invaded by forces wholly alien to personal being, political forces of which the worst is nuclear threat. In the same way, the landscape belongs to us and yet it does not. This concrete place we share is also a site on the nuclear grid. And when, therefore, Emerson tells us that "Every appearance in nature corresponds to some state of mind," we must inquire not only What state of mind? but also Whose mind?

No doubt the crews in the bombers are bored. And no doubt bureaucratic haggling keeps the commander of the base in Rome bogged down in mindless detail. The chiefs in the Pentagon, on the other hand, definitely share a state of mind which must, now and then, get rather dizzy with the glamour of their global strategy. What the Russians have in mind we don't know. But for all of them, we and the landscape are expendable; to think that way, after all, is their job. We cannot say, then, that the landscape corresponds to their minds and to ours in the same way. Rather, what expresses their state of mind, provokes and negates our own. In a traditional landscape, points of correspondence for us would be, among other things, the sky's infinity and the sense of permanence arising from the land itself. But exactly this kind of metaphor-making has been undermined by the transformation of the landscape into a sector on the grid. Or we might look at it this way: the military state of mind becomes an alien element *in* the landscape as we behold it, the B-52's, the proximity of the missile site, the grid and its planners. These forces have broken into our world, they have defiled its integrity, and the new points of correspondence between ourselves and the landscape are the condition of vulnerability and the threat of terminal defacement. Self and world, nature and landscape, everything exists in itself *and* as acceptable loss on the nuclear grid.

I've gone on at length about the landscape in my part of the country to suggest what Emerson's poetic principle — "Every appearance in nature corresponds to some state of mind" — might mean in the nuclear age. Every person has his or her own place, of course, and in a country as vast as ours the variety of landscape must be nearly infinite. The kinds of personal vision to which a landscape corresponds must also, then, be fairly limitless. But all vision converges in the fact that every landscape is part of the nuclear grid. I have the air base in Rome to remind me of this, whereas people living in, say, New York City are reminded by the city itself — its status as a prime target; the difficulty of maintaining life-support systems, water, energy, even in normal times; traffic's five o'clock entrapment every afternoon, not to mention the way the city is mocked by officials in Washington who suggest that in the event of an alert, nine million people will please evacuate the area. Then too, there are the nuclear power plants nearby; these are also targets, and when hit will spout radiation like the fourth of July. The citizenry can always avail itself of shovels, as another Washington wit has proposed, but no, there's no real hope. So that landscape too has its message.

Meanwhile, poets write about "marshes, lakes and woods, Sweet Emma of Preservation Hall, a Greek lover, an alchemist, actresses, fairy tales, canning peaches in North Carolina," stuff like that, to quote from the ad for a recent anthology. The apology for poems of this kind (triviality aside) is that by celebrating modest moments of the human spectacle — little snaps of wonder, bliss or pain — poetry implicitly takes its stand against nuclear negation. To say Yes to life, this argument goes, automatically says No to the Bomb. And yes, a grain of truth sprouts here. I expect many among us read poetry that way in any case. The upshot, however, is that poets can go on producing their vignettes of self, pleased to be fighting the good fight without undue costs — except *the* cost, which is the enforced superficiality, the required avoidance of our deeper dismay.

Nuclear threat engenders cynicism, despair, allegiance to a mystique of physical force, and to say No to such destructive powers requires an enormously vehement Yes to life and human value. What's called for, in fact, is the kind of poetry we once named "great," and my suspicion is that today the will to greatness is absent. Great poems, Wordsworth's or Whitman's for example, confront their times; they face and contain their own negation. The human spirit draws its strength from adversity, and so do poems. Examples like *The Prelude* and *Song of Myself* incorporate and thereby transcend that which, if they ignored it, would surely cancel their capacity for final affirmation. And having mentioned poems of this calibre, I might also add that the "American sublime," as critics call it, has been missing in our poetry at least since late Stevens. The sublime, as observers like Burke and Kant and Schopenhauer insist, arises from terror, terror beheld and resisted, the terror of revolution for Wordsworth, of the abyss for Whitman, of nuclear annihilation for any poet today who would make a language to match our extremity.

I can see, though, why we try to avoid what we know. Terror will flare up suddenly, a burst of flame in the chest, and then there is simply no strength. Other times the mind goes blank in disbelief. The temptation to retreat is always with us, but where can we go, where finally? Sometimes I let it all recede, let silence be enough, and go for a walk through the fields and apple hedge above my house. The horizon then is remarkably clear, the sky is still its oldest blue. Overhead, the planes are half a hemisphere ahead of their thunder. It's hard not to think of them as beautiful, sometimes; humankind took so long to get up there. I wind my way through milkweed in the meadow and remember how Emerson, crossing an empty field, felt glad to the brink of fear. We know what he means, the elation that sweeps through us at such moments. And then I think of Osip Mandelstam and an old Russian proverb; life, he wrote, is not a walk across a field. We know what he means too, the inhuman hardship of centuries, the modern horror of being stalked to death. But it's all of this, isn't it? the grimness and the glory. Why should we think to keep them apart? We fear, maybe, that dread will undermine our joy, and often it does. To keep them wed is poetry's job. And now that the big salvations have failed us, the one clear thing is that we live by words.

Pressures

As things are now going, the peace
we seem to be making will be a peace
of oil, a peace of gold, a peace of
shipping, a peace in brief...without
moral purpose or human interest.
— Archibald MacLeish
Poet and Assistant Secretary of State

All the new thinking is about loss.
In this it resembles all the old thinking.
— Robert Hass

Sharon Doubiago

Ground Zero

1.

We met on an evening in July
in one of the old taverns of this town,
two poets, unable to write, newly arrived,
hunted and haunted. For me,
the escape. For you,
the return.

You said you would show me
the Olympic Peninsula.

The road was overgrown.
In the headlights of your car I cleared the trees.
The cabin was vandalized, gutted,
the twenty-six oddshaped windows
opening onto the Straits, Canada and all the northern sky
shot out. The sink, the pump, the stoves,
even the doors, stolen.
You wandered around, then out to the deck,
seeming to forget me in the debris.

Victoria, the only human light,
shimmered on the foreign shore.
I heard the groan of a fishing boat below the bluff,
a strange cry from the woods, like a woman,
your ex-wife, the children. — *meaning some other
commitment*

We lay on a narrow mattress in the loft,
amidst bullet shells, beer cans, mold and glass,
the cold, hard bed of delinquent teenagers.

The moon was a broken boat through the bullet shattered
    skylight.
We told each other.
First words. I said
one night stand. You said ground zero.
I said I lost my children, my lover.

You said submarine, fucking vandals.
I said kids with no place to go, kids forbidden
to love. You said holocaust. Apocalypse.
I pulled you over on me. The volcano erupted.
The world turned to ash. I screamed
love cannot be gutted.
The moon, the stars, the giant trees watched
through a bullet hole.

2.

You moved in, installed sink, stoves, water pump.
Sixty oddshaped windows. You sat here
pissed as the eagle that stared from the bluff,
the greasepen numbers on the glass around your brooding head
like cabala, some secret military code.
When I visited, I felt a vandal.
When I left you cried deserted.
Betrayed.

In November I moved in.
Sheetrock. Yellow paint named Sunlight.
My white dog, Moonlight.
I said I'd stay until the place
became a landscape in my dreams.
By moon's light through the bullet hole
I began to write.
Your words: The Duckabush, The Dosiewallips, The Hamma
    Hamma.

It snowed in December.
You followed Coyote's tracks to the log where he slept.
A trapper came on the deep path.
He had Coyote. He gave you his card.
He boasted he'd get the rest.
He hinted that for money he could get them for you.

You were not easy to love.
You couldn't speak. Your tongue was cut out.
I left, screaming down the interstate,
avoiding the road over the mountains
to my old, equally beautiful, home.

You wrote me. One Trident submarine equals
two thousand and forty Hiroshimas.

In the cities I was weighted with cedar, an inland sea,
like provisions carried on my back.
Friends I'd always respected said
they couldn't live without culture.
I was weighted with the culture of eagle, coyote, people
like weather, like stars, functions of nature, not
human will, money, concrete.

3.

I came back to study the language of gulls,
the stories they scream to each other
as they fly off their sanctuary,
Protection Island.

You pulled me up the stairs.
Beyond your head I watched the moon through the bullet hole.
You said six layers of mountains
from the road, you said rivers
without end. You quoted Rilke's
Neptune of the blood and his terrible trident.
You said Trident
submarine. You said
zero.

I came back to stare back at Eagle,
to cut, carry, and chop our firewood,
to piss in the tall fern, to shit
in *the first little house you ever built*.
I came back and broke my habit at last
of the electric typewriter.
I came back to our cruel and grinding poverty,
never enough kerosene, gasoline, postage, paper or pens.
We turned off the propane. It is so cold in our house
the little food on our shelves is naturally iced.

I came back to listen to the woods,
gull squawk and moandance of cedar, fir and alder,
the high scream of wind through the mouth of Haro,

Rosario, Deception Pass
where the ships disappear on the inward passage.
I came back to listen to your breath
as you sleep beside me. Poet. Your words.
Puma. Ish. Milosz. The children
who once lived here.

4.

You weighted me with your poems,
like provisions. I left, drove home.
My children were grown, gone.
Your words pulled me back.

We climb the stairs together.
The roof leaks, the cabin is for sale.
I say it is ours for now. Our one night stand,
our two hundred nights.

You tell me of this thing that is coming,
the deadliest weapon ever made.
Two football fields, four stories high.
Two thousand and forty Hiroshimas.

It can be anywhere in the world, undetected,
and hit its target within half a foot.
It can be anywhere in the world and no one,
not the President, not the Computer
will be able to find it.

One day soon it will enter the Straits of Juan de Fuca.
The most evil thing ever created
will float beneath our cabin, then down
the Hood Canal.

You say four hundred and eight cities
from a single submarine. You say
First Strike Weapon. You say
shoot out their silos. You say
U.S.S. Ohio.

5.

I came upon an old man
teaching his granddaughter and grandson
how to shoot.

I sat here alone.
The door banged open and four kids
burst in. Perfume, six packs, party clothes.
I think I frightened them
as much as they frightened me.

On clear days the islands rise up.
San Juan. Lopez. Orcas, white skyscrapers
on Vancouver. How many ships, my love,
have come and gone since we came? How many whales,
eagles, coyotes and gulls?
I finished my epic poem here.
You finished *The Straits*.

Every night the human city
shimmers and beckons on the Canadian shore.
Every night of one whole week
the sky wove and unwove
the rainbow flags of all the north
delicately over us. The Aurora
Borealis.

Two seasons of snow, now the season of light again.
My one night stand, our four hundred
nights.

I saw car lights descend Protection Island
to the water.
The leaks in the roof washed away
my nightwritten words.
We saw six killer whales
rise and fall through the water.
You said my rejected poems. I said
your smallminded editors. I said
I can almost understand now
what the gulls are saying.

6.

My dreams take place on an inland sea,
a land soaked in silver shadows and blue.
We are traveling to the heart of the continent.
We are looking for a room to rent. We are having a baby.
We are building a house.
You say unrecognized. Unpublished. I say just
wait. You say holocaust. You say apocalypse. I say
love.

Once you went with me.
Once you came for me.

We climb the loft together. This, you say
is your home now. This northwest corner. This last place
we can run.

This bed of outlaws, circle of mountains, finger
of glacier water, dark sun of winter behind
Mt. Olympus.

7.

Light shoots through the skylights.
Twenty full moons awake us.
Moonlight sleeps below by the fire, cries from nightmare.
The Manx, the Siamese watch us through the bullet hole.
We lie in terror,
watch the giant trees arch and blow over us,
rain and wind so fierce
we wait without words to be crushed.
Finally I say maybe we should leave. You say
where would we go?
You say death like a storm that might / might not
blow over. You say Puma.
I say Tatoosh means Thunderbird.
Like Phoenix, like rebirth.
You say the last crisis is not death,
but how to be beautiful.
How to die
beautifully.

8.

Say the word Hiroshima.
Reflect on its meaning for one second.
Say and understand Hiroshima again.
Say and understand Hiroshima two thousand and forty times.

Assuming you are able to understand Hiroshima in
one second, you will be able to understand Trident
in thirty four minutes. That's one Trident submarine.
To understand the destructive power of the whole
Trident fleet, it will take you seventeen hours
devoting one second to each Hiroshima. *

9.

The real estate agents are lost on Old Dump Road.
Coyote yelps. The last hunter shoots.

The kids break through the woods
still looking for the party.
I throw open the window. "Here's your bed!
Come join us! We've kept it warm for you!"
You always pull me back to weep in your arms, where

are my teenagers?

10.

The volcano erupted. The world turned to ash.
Now the planets line up: *six hundred days and nights*.
The sun comes north
falls into the mouth of the Straits.
Rhododendron. Honeysuckle. Calypso. Trillium.
The stunted shrub blazes up
like a flaming heart.

And snow circle of mountains! Ring of fire!
Rainier, Mt. Baker, Glacier Peak, St. Helens!
Olympic Home of the Gods: *Sappho, Makah, Joyce, Quinault.*
Shi Shi, La Push, Ozette, Kalaloch.
How many nights, my love, how many poems, my great poet
we have awakened

*from Jim Douglass's *Lightning East and West*.

to the low moan of a fishing boat,
someone's voice, almost,
heard in the trees

It has already left. It is on its way.
It is coming around from the other side of the continent.
The date is a secret.

It will enter the mouth of the Straits,
then slip down the Hood Canal.
It will move beneath your cabin.
It will come through your windows.

You will be anywhere in the world
and it will find you.

for Michael Daley
March 25, 1982

21

Stephen Dunn

The Cocked Finger

I don't know why it is
that the bomb, the end,
seems closer. For years
I've lived with it, *them*,
that incredible dosage
of destruction, and I've sat
in livingrooms and discussed living
things, took vacations,
raised my kids as if
the future was what, in spite
of everything, they might enter
like aspirants, not like
lemmings. But now
on our side, as if there were
a side when it comes
to imagining the end of sides,
there's a nice, simple man
and perhaps only a nice man
could press such a button,
believing he was saving
the world for niceness.
And on the other side
there's a terrible dullness
and the dull are always
dangerous, home alone too much
with the latest equipment.
                    God, once I cared
if you existed, conjured prayers
just in case.
But it no longer matters —
there's History which is larger
than you, the bully
who knows every pressure
point, every weakness,
eager for the next moment.
I've gotten used to the rapes,
the murders. I eat dinner

22

and watch them on Channel Six
and nothing shocks me,
not even kindness,
not even, though I'm afraid,
the bomb.
The finger that might
touch it off is cocked
like an apostrophe
on the wrong side of a possessive,
an error so obvious
almost everyone can see it.
           Now here comes
History, pretending
it just wants to be understood.
It's begun to breathe hard,
and there's no record of it
ever being a lover, nor exhausted
from all that it's done.

Eric Larsen

Writing and Nostalgia: Hiding in the Past

"Can't repeat the past?" he cried incredulously. "Why of course you can!"

— The Great Gatsby

Like a lot of other people, I have listened with a close interest — as student, teacher, and writer — to the many claims that have been made in the last decade or so for the special vitality and plentiful robustness of current American writing. Some of these claims (I'll cite a few in a minute) are broad, sweeping, and quite spectacular: our age of writing, they say, is the finest age of writing in the nation that there's ever been. Certainly this idea, especially coming from the mouths of responsible and respected people, is a compelling one, and certainly it would be quite nice to believe its truth. Unfortunately, though, for me at least, that just isn't possible.

Generalizations are a risky business, I know, but when I look at it carefully, much current writing gives me cause for a good measure of serious doubt. I would like to be more celebratory than this, and I make such a remark with my eyes open to qualification. Nor do I speak as one of those so gloomy and disillusioned, at least not yet, as to label the whole age a failure —gripped hopelessly by paralysis, mass passivity, and the mental sloth of the television culture. Things are bad, it's true, but not that bad. And yet, speaking of doubts, I do suspect that there may be a special significance in a serious literature that fails, sometimes ostentatiously, to grow away from its own inherited conventions, that allows itself willingly to drift toward the anti-intellectual, and that appears to arise out of, more than anything else, a deep and craving hunger—a nostalgia—for the past.

I'll go so far as to say that one of the most pervasive criteria by which literary excellence finds itself judged just now may very well be nostalgia. In the popular culture, as everyone knows who watches television, goes to the movies, visits flea markets, or shops in Georgetown boutiques, nostalgia has taken on the dimensions almost of a chronic condition. Less often, though, is it observed to exist in what we think of as the intellectual culture, including the literary culture. And yet there are signs of its presence there, too, waiting to be seen.

Nostalgia reveals itself in writing—or hides itself—in a number of ways, and it lives just as contentedly within works of "quality" or "excellence" as it does within those of mediocrity or even outright trashiness. In the latter—in the so-called "genre" romances, for example—anybody can see it, since it tends to be obvious, superficial, and transparent. In "serious" writing, though, it can be a more elusive quality, partly because all aspects of serious writing, including the use of the past, tend, obviously, to be more refined, subtle, and complex.

Even so, it can be said in general that nostalgia in serious writing is betokened by one kind or other of aesthetic or emotional conservatism, whether in form, tone, subject matter, or attitude. Such conservatism is not in itself a bad thing; half of the great writers in the history of the world, after all, have been conservatives in these ways, and the true artist, however innovative — Virgil no less than Jane Austen — is always a conserver of past traditions. But such conservatism becomes nostalgia at a certain very important point: it does so at the point when the artist ceases to be aware of that conservatism as a *tool* of his art, and when he accepts it, instead, as a source of meaning in itself. When this happens (the author, of necessity, unaware of what he has done), then conservatism is transformed suddenly into a kind of reactionism: the artist is no longer using the past, but instead he is returning to it.

Such a turning to the past, of course, can be done in differing degrees and manners, with differing purposes, and with differing degrees of success. But the *using* of the past is one thing, while a nostalgic falling *into* the past is clearly another; and it seems indisputable, if nothing else, that just now a strong nostalgic impulse plays an important part in much of our current and most praised writing.

Ambitious, serious, and often popular books as different in their aims and in their success as *Sleepless Nights* and *Sophie's Choice* are both deeply serious in their uses of nostalgia and turning to the past. Joyce Carol Oates' *Bellefleur*, emblem of popular interest in the Gothic and in the "old," tirelessly re-creates long-gowned love stories and demonic Faulknerian heroes. In *Emmeline*, Judith Rossner searches for meaning in the nineteenth-century mills and boarding houses of Lowell, Massachusetts, while E.L. Doctorow follows the coolly faceted entertainments of *Ragtime* by evoking the 1930's with the same museum pleasures of arrested detail. Other disparate books, like John Casey's *An American Romance*, with its revisited ruralism and extended analogues to the coming-of-age elements of Scott Fitzgerald or D.H. Lawrence, or books like *Going After Cacciato*, with its structure of earnestly wistful escapism — these books, too, have the yearning evocation of nostalgia and the modes of the past in the flavor of their pages.

I know that it's nothing new, and that, in itself, it isn't necessarily bad either. Nostalgia, after all, has had its vital place in literature from at least as far back as *The Iliad* (there was a time, sings Homer, when men were heroes). Coming a lot closer to home, the evocative lyricism of *Look Homeward, Angel* is nothing if not nostalgic, and there may never have been books written by mortals that are more nostalgic or born more intensely out of the spirit of nostalgia than treasured works like *The Sun Also Rises* or *The Great Gatsby*. And yet there is a difference, and I think it's a difference that has to do with the relationship between the past and the future in our time. For a number of reasons, the age we live in has lost its ability to draw people toward the future with a sense of vitality, security, or hope. One result of this fact is that what comes to seem most desirable, and most meaningful also, is not the promise or release of a cleansed future, but the security and comfort of a known past.

Those earlier books by Hemingway, Fitzgerald, and Thomas Wolfe, as well as many others like them—one thinks of *Absalom! Absalom!*, *Winesburg, Ohio*, *My Antonia*, *In Our Time*—were written in a time that was still capable of change, that was capable still of conceiving its own future; and their nostalgia was capable of transformation therefore into a symbolism that acclaimed the possibility, even the desirability, of that future. Nostalgia in the writing of our own time, however, is something different. It tends to look only backward. It is a closing up and a withdrawal from the probabilities of the future, rather than a long glance backward before a releasing step forward. Nostalgia in our own writing has a paradoxically determined will-lessness and lack of boldness to it (however intense the need may have been to bring it into existence), a quality often of prior resignation and of an excessive reliance upon the aura, tone, or achievement of past works. There is in it a suggestion of being weighed-upon by something empty, paralyzed, or malign in the world of its own future, and this suggestion is accompanied by a sometimes subtle quality of resigned passivity, a suggestion of being in flight from that future, of seeking asylum in the echoes and aesthetic vocabularies of the past. In extreme cases there is in fact a wistfulness for the past so pervasive and so numbing of perception that it creates a failure to see clearly, as any art must, what the true material of its own present age really is. Considering these matters, I think it's possible, whatever its praiseworthy and workmanlike aspects, that much of our newer writing may never have been in a worse or more pitiable situation.

There are numerous arguments precisely to the contrary, I know. I've already mentioned some of the claims that our nation has been for some time now in the midst of a vast, pluralistic literary renaissance, that we are witness to a burgeoning of creative talent, that the future is—well, that the future is great writing, and lots of it. Departments of Literature across the country are effectively being turned into Departments of Writing as the reading of literature gives way to the writing of it. The National Endowment for the Arts, even before the Reagan Administration slashed its budget, lamented that there was not enough money to reward all the deserving talent in the country, and people of high stature in publishing and the arts have concurred about the renaissance. Some years ago, Theodore Solotaroff wrote in *The American Review* (now, however, defunct) that there is "a major outcropping of literary talent in America. To my mind, there are more accomplished writers at work in America today than at any time in our history." And Joyce Carol Oates, in the prize volume of short stories she edited with Shannon Ravenel two years ago, provided an echo of Solotaroff: "More good work is being done by more gifted writers than ever before."

However well-intended and sincere they may be, I sense a bandwagon somewhere behind statements like these. The claims are high ones, and, as I said earlier, I don't entirely believe them. That a great number of people are writing is without doubt—the nation is flooded by "creative" writing, university writing, "grassroots" writing, prison writing, community workshop writing, NEA-supported writing—but the significance and real nature of this output, it seems to me, are other matters and deserve a closer look.

There are today, as in any time, a certain number of noteworthy, significant, or independent literary achievements (and some of these I'm sure we don't even know about yet); but it seems to me that our current literary industriousness as a whole is expressive less of an unprecedented cultural growth or genuine renaissance than it is of something quite other: something which may not be excellent, which is in no way revolutionary, and which has to do at least in large part with the ambiguously unsatisfying nature of the time we live in. What the new writing reveals is less a major renaissance than an affluent and literate (if not terribly cultured or deeply educated) society's predominantly middle class attempt to react against the sense of banality, individual powerlessness, and paralyzing uneventfulness in the world surrounding it.

There is nothing either ignoble or culpable about a reaction such as this, and I'm not going to claim that there is. But by the same token, I don't think there is anything altogether cynical either in seeking to identify some of the real—rather than the more popular and idealistic—reasons why so many people are suddenly making that reaction by becoming writers. These reasons, I suspect, can be distilled into three, and I don't intend them to sound flippant. Still, it is clear that more people than "ever before" have the *time* to be writers. It is clear, too, that more people than ever before are *encouraged* to be writers, for reasons ranging from the genuinely cultural to the emotionally therapeutic to the toting up of lots of college credits. And, finally, one additional matter of numbers: because the nation's population itself is greater than ever before, more *people* than ever before tend to live their lives, however understandably, with the growing sense that they want something, in the seeming paralysis and banality of the world around them, to be meaningful. That meaningful thing often becomes writing.

So what's the problem? The problem is that in the very act of turning to literature—and this is the aspect of much current writing that I suspect is the most significant—many writers, among them some who are well known and highly successful, tend less to confront or embrace the reality of their own present world than they tend, with whatever high aims, to seek escape from it. The practise of writing, in other words, becomes a means not by which to enter the reality of the world itself and translate that experience into art, but a means by which to leave the uncomforting or unsatisfying truths of that world—and of its future—behind. Serious writing, in a word, and very possibly with the highest aims, becomes escapist. Most frequently in literary expression such escape takes the form, whether in subject, manner, tone, or literary form, of a return to the past (the act of writing itself is a reassuringly old-fashioned habit), with the result, as Alfred Kazin lamented not long ago, that "a whole dimension of present literature is occupied by nostalgia."

Serious writing is never easy, and yet the age we live in is an especially difficult one to write about significantly or accurately; ours is a time particularly well calculated to throw writers off the beam of truth or to frustrate them into traveling down attractive blind alleys. Susan Sontag, writing in 1965 about science fiction movies and the threat of the world's end through nuclear holocaust, made the following remark; surely it is no less true now than it was a decade and a half ago. "Ours is indeed an age of extremity," she wrote. "For we live under continual threat of two equally fearful, but seemingly opposed, destinies: unremitting banality and inconceivable terror."

She went on:

> It is fantasy, served out in large rations by the popular arts, which allows most people to cope with these twin specters. For one job that fantasy can do is to lift us out of the unbearably humdrum and to distract us from terrors—real or anticipated—by an escape into exotic, dangerous situations which have last-minute happy endings. But another of the things that fantasy can do is to normalize what is psychologically unbearable, thereby inuring us to it. In one case, fantasy beautifies the world. In the other, it neutralizes it.

Sontag, of course, was talking about movies, not literature, and she was talking about fantasy, not nostalgia. Still, obvious parallels exist between her observations and the observations a person might make today about current writing. It is true that writers today, just like movie-makers and all other human beings, live in a world caught between banality and terror. And it is true also that nostalgia is itself a form of fantasy, a form that happens to provide, with its own particular effectiveness, "an escape into [the] exotic."

To put it more bluntly, the past serves effectively as an escape from the present, just as fantasy in movies serves as an escape from the unconfrontable. More than this, however, the past offers its services in a particularly cunning and perhaps misleading way to the insufficiently alert literary practitioner. Because it is attractive, because it is exotic, and because it is considered generally to possess an innate significance, the past carries with it a considerable and highly available prestige. Thus a person can hide comfortably within its substance and form, can turn his back on the present world altogether and escape quite blindly into the warm folds of history's flesh, yet can still *seem* (even to himself) to be engaging, and with a correspondingly high degree of significance, in nothing less than the world's reality itself. It may very well be this principle—the comfort of the familiar—that to a large extent sustains much writing today, a desire for things as they were.

Not only among writers but also among the general culture, this lure toward the past as meaningful fantasy is a good deal stronger now than normally, or perhaps than ever. Not long ago, the historian John Lukacs observed that "There exists now in the United States a widespread appetite for history—more exactly, for physical and mental reminders of the past—that in the entire history of this country has no precedent." As evidence of this appetite, Lukacs mentions entertainment successes as various as "social-historical soap operas like 'Upstairs Downstairs,'" popular histories "like *The Guns of August, Eleanor and Franklin, The Day Lincoln Was Shot, The Longest Day*," as well as works like *Ragtime* and *Roots* and "Mailer's and Capote's recent books," these last four being examples of "a new kind of book," a "hybrid historical genre [that] now threatens to overwhelm the genre of the novel."

And yet this desire for the very touch and feel of the past, Lukacs points out, has occurred at a time when the teaching of history has all but disappeared from American schools and when the profession of historian, narrowed to "fashionable practices like quantification, psycho-history, and the preoccupation with 'timely'...subjects," has been reduced to the level of "a social science." Lukacs is clear in explaining why such a discrepancy exists between popular interest in history and serious practice of it, and he makes a distinction that is crucial, also, to an understanding of what nostalgia really is. "This appetite," he says, "has developed at a time when much of the teaching of history has been thoughtlessly and shamefully abandoned by those responsible for it. Historical thinking may have entered the very blood of people; but the *awareness* of historical thinking has not entered their minds."

The widespread turning toward the past that is now observable, in other words, may not in fact be a result of thinking or of thought at all, but rather a matter of desire: the result of a desire that is visceral and emotional rather than intellectual, an unintellectualized yearning to retreat altogether from the shallow banalities, the disorienting terrors, and the wan, thin enmities of the present world. The past, to put it simply, is more appealing than the present, let alone the ominous threat that is the future. And people can desire physically to return to it due to a very explicit, precise, and, above all, non-intellectual belief. "They are attracted," Lukacs writes, "by the idea that the past is *real*."

Following Lukacs's observation, it becomes increasingly clear that nostalgia has nothing in common with historical thinking, with the study of history, or with a clear understanding of the purposes of history. History, after all, will never teach the one thing that nostalgia inevitably teaches. Nostalgia alone, when grown pathological, sufficiently intense, and deeply enough ingrained, will lead its followers directly to this remarkable and remarkably false conclusion: that the past is *real*.

It is for these reasons, at least in part, that much recent literary judgement — both of critics and of authors — is excessively adulatory, naively enthusiastic, and frequently myopic in its estimation of the real significance of much current literary work. If the past is deemed to be real, certainly it is a corollary belief that it must possess also a *significance* equal in kind and degree to that of any other reality; therefore, an immersion in the past must be as significant as an immersion in the present. And if this is so, then the very notion of literary judgment itself must undergo an important change. There was a time when works that copied or were enslaved by the past or by past tradition, whether in their subject matter or in their literary forms or manner, were criticized for being archaic, derivative, or hollowly duplicative. Now, however, such works might as likely find themselves praised instead for their achievement, workmanship, and ambition — simply for the wonder of their existence.

Once this extent of aesthetic and intellectual confusion has been reached, there is little the literary critic can do except try to identify and lament the self-deceptions, skewed reasoning, and false evaluations that must inevitably result. Increasingly, however, to do exactly this is to work against the grain not only of commercial and popular but also of academic literary tastes. Reading serious critical praise for a book like Joyce Carol Oates's *Bellefleur*, for example, is unnerving to a reader who finds it to have little literary significance, seeing in it the product of an imagination passive and uncritical in its acceptance and repossession of the traditions, forms, modes, and rhythms of the past literature from which, however industriously and with whatever eager aesthetic naivete, it has taken its nourishment. Lethargic at root, passive and accepting even in its inheritance of verbal prolixity and in its nervous veneer of seeming linguistic intensity, it is a book, it seems to me, whose essential purpose finally can be none other than to duplicate what has already been done, and therefore to occupy, fill up, perhaps endeavor to stop, the dreadful passage of mean and vacant time.

"Ours is, doom sayers to the contrary," *Bellefleur*'s author wrote in the introduction to her *Best American Short Stories* volume in 1979, "not only a highly literate age: it is also a highly *literary* age. More people are writing, and writing well, than ever before in our history." She added: "we are living in an era of particularly well crafted work, whether fiction or poetry."

Perhaps so. And yet here is an indication of precisely what I have been suggesting, or part of what I have been suggesting: once again, the *fact* of writing is applauded, the *doing* of it is praised, while other questions—the purpose, meaning, or significance of such writing, for example—seem not to arise or to be conceived of as having a greater importance. Literary attitudes of this kind in their extreme form undoubtedly have numerous origins (they are, for one thing, highly democratic and seem to be intensely "fair"; I suspect also that writing workshops, with their necessary praise for the writing of dedicated neophytes, may have a certain influence), but I am speaking here primarily of nostalgia, and, as I've tried to suggest, that includes nostalgia also for past *forms* of expression. The volume of prize stories in which Oates made the remarks I have quoted is (like other volumes of its kind) a compendium not so much of exhaustion (there's hard work in it) as it is a compendium of a subtle not-looking at the present. With exceptions (stories by Alice Munro and Jayne Anne Phillips, for example), the book is content by and large to offer imitativeness in the name of the aesthetically significant. Implicitly praising a kind of paradoxically assertive literary passivity, the book offers laurels for what appears to be an emerging choice to write and live within the inherited aesthetics, literary forms, moods, and feelings of the past.

The piece in the book that perhaps illustrates this tendency best is William Styron's "Shadrach," a childhood reminiscence set in the year 1935. Other stories in the volume, some skillful and others embarrassingly amateurish, bespeak the past or an aesthetic retreat to the past in a number of ways: there is a weak story by a dead author (Flannery O'Connor), a sentimental boyhood narrative by Louis D. Rubin, Jr., an imitation of Samuel Beckett by Donald Barthelme, classroom imitations of Ernest

Hemingway by Sean Virgo and Rolf Yngve more suited to student magazines than to a national prize anthology, wistful glances into the past by Peter LaSalle, Rosellen Brown, Saul Bellow. Some of these stories are moving, some successful, others inadequate. Some use the past well, while others seem to me to be used by the past. William Styron's piece, one of these latter, possesses an interest for showing perhaps most clearly the capacity of nostalgia, when manifested in inherited literary form, not only to turn the eyes and judgment of the writer away from the world of the present, but effectively to distort truth itself.

The story concerns the Dabneys, a tidewater family of white trash descended obscurely from a rich landowning past. To them one day, emblem of this distant history, there appears a ninety-nine year old ex-slave named Shadrach, who has walked from Alabama in order "to die and be buried on 'Dabney ground.'" He does die, but he is prevented by state law from being buried on the small remnant of land still owned by the Dabneys. The story ends with Mr. Dabney—after a moment of frustrated rage during which he shouts that "'It's life that's fearsome! *Life!*'"—concluding that the old man won't "know the difference" no matter where he is buried. "'When you're dead nobody knows the difference. Death ain't much.'"

The story's narrator, ten years old in 1935, is infatuated with the Dabneys and filled with a sense of religious piety toward Shadrach. He "loved and envied the whole Dabney tribe," envies their "sheer teeming multitude," praises their naturalness, absence of intellectuality, and poverty:

> I envied their abandoned slovenliness, their sour unmade beds, their roaches, the cracked linoleum on the floor, the homely cur dogs leprous with mange that foraged at will through house and yard. My perverse longings were—to turn around a phrase unknown at the time—downwardly mobile. Afflicted at the age of ten by *nostalgie de la boue*, I felt deprived of a certain depravity. I was too young to know, of course, that one of the countless things of which the Dabneys were victim was the Great Depression.

Styron's nostalgia seems clearly to be nostalgia for the sense of meaning and significance possessed by the lives of the Dabneys. Whether the boy narrator, half a century later, would still hold the Dabneys—with their poverty, ignorance, and squalor—in the same regard is a question unanswered by the story, which gives no indication of the boy's adult attitude and does not distance itself significantly from his ten year old view. Accordingly, the idealizing impulse in the story—whether Styron's or the boy's—continues. When Shadrach appears, the boy is reminded of the Old Testament patriarchs, "whose names flooded my mind in a Sunday school litany," and at this time he takes a closer look at the old man:

> ...cataracts clouded his eyes like milky cauls, the corneas swam with rheum. Yet...above the implacable sweet grin there were flickers of wise recognition. His presence remained worrisomely Biblical; I felt myself drawn to him with an almost devout compulsion, as if he were the prophet Elijah sent to bring truth, light, the Word. The shiny black mohair mail-order suit he wore was baggy and grayed, streaked with dust; the cuffs hung loose, and from one of the ripped ankle-high clodhoppers protruded a naked black toe. Even so, the presence was thrillingly ecclesiastical and fed my piety.

It ought to be eminently clear even from this amount of quoting that "Shadrach" is a "well written" and "well crafted" story, and yet those merits are unable to change the fact that it is also a story deeply thwarted by the pulse of nostalgia that beats in its heart. Certainly it is a piece that seems ambitious in its aims—throwing itself backward half a century to examine, re-enter, and assess matters that are not, by any known measure, of mean significance. And yet, regardless of its apparent boldness and of its subject matter itself—nothing less than poverty, ignorance, squalor, slavery, and death—to read "Shadrach" is, surprisingly, to read a story of wistful pleasures, of contentedness, of a sweet kind of softness, above all of harmlessness, of an abstract mood of gentle meaningfulness, a story where pain, in the end, isn't really so very great. The story and its historic subject matter seem, when one thinks back through the piece, hardly to have anything to do with one another, hardly to be related at all. John Lukacs might be able to explain why this is the case: while "Shadrach" is a narrative on a historical subject, he might tell us, it is a narrative that does not think historically.

A meaningful or significant backward-looking narrative, I suspect, does not as a rule have as its first aim to seduce the past, but rather to study it; it may seek to reconstruct the past, even lovingly, but it harbors no delusions about wishing, as the prime and salient purpose of the writing, to re-enter it. This is true of the novels of Thomas Wolfe or the stories of Sherwood Anderson, for example, of the stories in *Dubliners* or in *In Our Time*, of *The Great Gatsby*, of historical narratives at novel length as different as those by Marguerite Yourcenar and Mary Renault, as varied as Robert Graves's Claudius novels, Thornton Wilder's *The Ides of March*, or Gore Vidal's *Julian, Burr*, or *1876*. To seek to re-enter the past is to seek escape. To seek to alter the past in order to make it desirable — and not to call this exercise fantasy — is to deceive.

In "Shadrach," the past is not so much studied, is not so much re-created in order for it to be seen more clearly, as it is idealized, dramatically and symbolically yearned for, and this yearning informs the whole fabric of the narrative. The absence of a tone of historical irony in "Shadrach" (except for its few "then and now" brush strokes, themselves mainly nostalgic); the blurring of significant distancing devices between the narrator and the author; the comfortably familiar nature of its literary stance; its avuncular and deeply nostalgic tone; its choice of subject matter itself; its involvement with the metaphors of religious adoration of symbols of the past — all of these suggest the extent of the desire. It is because of this desire above all that the story thus idealizes the past: renders it, however inauthentically, as being at its heart essentially harmless, painless, and rich, with a soft, redolent, and wistfully desirable texture of meaning. The past feels *safe*. Through this kind of romanticizing, the story achieves its greatest distortion, for it effectively serves to falsify the actual nature of real squalor, suffering, and ignorance, whether of the past or of the present. Posing as reality, the story is fantasy. Posing as history, it sanitizes the past. Pretending to realism, it makes its escape into the false exotic.

Some might argue that I place too much weight on a single story that just happens to look at the past through rose-colored glasses, as myriad other stories, to one degree or another, do. But that is part of the point. "Shadrach" is important less for itself than for the familiar impulses it reveals, for its similarities to other representative current writing, including Styron's own — long narratives and short, well known and obscure, commercially successful and "purely" literary. Desire for the past is a dangerous tyranny, as history can teach us, and yet in pieces of writing such as "Shadrach," however skillfully disguised the fact may seem to be, there is an almost complete absence of real historical sense, of *thinking* that could be called historical. Such a piece is not a glass through which to see the past more clearly, nor through which to sense the truth of our own world more precisely, with fresh aesthetic awareness, or with greater courage. Rather, such a story is emotional fantasy clothed as serious work. It is a soft falling away. It is a swoon.

I turn in closing to John Gardner, since, in his literary criticism, he is the writer who has gone a step farther and has sought to turn the impulse of nostalgia into not only an emotional but a moral crusade. In his response to certain unarguably authentic dilemmas of life in the present, Gardner has evolved an a-historical literary aesthetic that not only turns emotionally to the past but that, in certain important respects, willfully abandons the perceiving and judgmental capacities of the intellect altogether.

Never as specific as Susan Sontag was in identifying the exact nature of the emotional and aesthetic *impasse* faced by dwellers in the contemporary world, Gardner has, nevertheless, very clearly felt the frustration of that world, especially as revealed in its aesthetics. In *On Moral Fiction*, he explains that an element of vital importance is absent from the world of the present, making "nearly everything that passes for art...tinny and commercial and often, in addition, hollow and academic." Starting from a position almost exactly opposite that of the literary optimists, Gardner's response to the situation is unselfconsciously impetuous and also explicit: he will argue, he says, both "by reason and by banging the table...for an old-fashioned view of what art is and what the fundamental business of critics ought therefore to be."

Others have written about the earnestness and zeal in Gardner's criticism, as well as about his effort—labored, serious, and frequently contradictory—to define exactly what morality (the element missing in modern art) actually *is* in writing. But more to the point here is to observe the intellectual sacrifice created by Gardner in his flight to the past. Baffled and enraged by the meretriciousness and hyper-intellectualism of the present world, he turns to an aesthetic past that he believes, however rightly or wrongly, to be more heroic and moral. In so turning—and this,

I think, is the more important part—he undertakes to shape a plan by which he will eliminate thought and intellect from the scheme of things altogether and replace them with new forces: feeling and vision. The cure thus becomes as lop-sided as the cause that gave rise to it.

At the beginning of *On Moral Fiction*, Gardner explains that "To understand a complex work of art, one must be something of an artist oneself," and from this point on he idealizes the artist, making of him a gifted visionary, and simultaneously denigrating all that is merely intellectual. He makes it clear that true art cannot be defined by people who use their minds and who think (and who think historically, one might add), but only by artistic visionaries; this is because "the artist's character —the whole complex of his ideas and emotions—is his final authority on what is, and what is not, art. Except insofar as they are really artists, critics have, finally, no authority at all."

That, then, is the first step, the creation, in repudiation of the intellect, of a kind of "visionary authoritarianism." Gardner carries the plan further in the second step, in which he denigrates intellectuals further by additionally exalting visionaries. Imbuing his argument with a flavor of religious messianism, he reveals that writers and artists, unlike thinkers and intellectuals, are in fact divine: they are "the sons of God."

Thus the artist is deified. Only a final step remains for the liquidation of the intellectual, and this last step, I think, is one indigenous to the purest type of nostalgist or romantic: the willful leaving of the real world behind in favor of another, superior, "dream" world. "Other things being equal," Gardner concludes, "the more intensely the artist imagines his dream world, the more fully he surrenders to it, the more passionate his devotion to capturing it in words, images, or music—or, to put it another way, the deeper his trance and the greater his divorce from ordinary reality—the greater is likely to be the effect of the artist's work on the reader, viewer, or listener."

The suggestion, then, is clear that intellect has been wholly overcome; and at this point, the chasm between intellect and feeling is so vast as to be unbridgeable. The floating, drug-like tone of phrases like these—"dream world," "surrender," "the deeper his trance," "divorce from ordinary reality"—make evident that what is being talked about, above all, are ideas not of the intellect, but of intense desire, of the senses, of the willed swoon into art as escape.

Eric Larsen

Gardner's critical voice has its roots historically in visionary messianism and in high romanticism, and it is a voice filled also with more recent echoes of the late 1960's cults of the sensually heightened and the hallucinatory. Its deep anti-intellectualism, of course, is quite clear. But its additional embracing of an aesthetic religiosity that implies or allows, if not outright advocates, the leaving of the real world behind—as being of a merely passing, secondary interest—seems to me at this point in history to be at best a radical archaism whose purpose in the name of art reveals itself to be essentially solipsistic and escapist, the end product perhaps of a variety of causes, but certainly among them a long-frustrated and radically unexamined nostalgic yearning for life in a world other than the one in which we live.

It's true, though, that Gardner's thinking possesses a kind of rambunctious inconsistency, and, in a review of *Bellefleur* at the time when that novel appeared, he espouses the real world once again long enough to have another word or two about people who live in it by attempting to use their minds. Joyce Carol Oates is a popular novelist, he says in that review, "because her stories are suspenseful...because her sex scenes are steamy and because when she describes a place you think you're there. Pseudo-intellectuals seem to hate that popularity and complain, besides, that she 'writes too much.' (For pseudo-intellectuals there are always too many books.)" Having thus suggested that good books are nothing but earthy composites of steamy sex, good descriptions, and suspense (Oates "is one of the great writers of our time"), Gardner returns again to his less earthly considerations. He says approvingly of Jedediah, *Bellefleur's* visionary mountain recluse, that he "becomes the instrument of the blind life force that, accidentally, indifferently, makes everything of value, makes everything beautiful by the simple virtue of its momentary existence." And Gardner then washes his hands of all intellectual responsibility for the maintenance of the world whatsoever by declaring that this accidental, indifferent, "blind life force" is in actuality none other than us, we ourselves, the people who live on earth. "Thanks to Jedediah," he concludes, "God goes on ceaselessly humming, discovering Himself. That is, in Miss Oates's vision, the reason we have to live and the reason life, however dangerous, can be a joy, once we understand our situation: We are God's body."

Given the brink of the frightful abyss to which we have so far brought our world, I am not comforted by the idea that it is we ourselves who are God, by whatever odd mishmash of Platonism, Christianity, archaic romantic mysticism and befuddled aesthetics we may have become so. Nor, I admit, do I find Gardner's explanation of the meaning of the literary soap-operatic *Bellefleur* a confidence-inspiring paradigm for the achievement of the best art of the late twentieth century: while God (Who is We) goes on blithely humming, paring His fingernails in a beatific, hallucinatory and backward-yearning stupor, the real world, with all alarms ringing loudly in its clear and present need for painstaking, alert, and intelligent attention, is set off between parenthetical commas ("however dangerous") and is allowed somehow to muddle along, to take care of itself, to find as if by divine and indifferent accident its own blind and dumb way.

And yet precisely this state of affairs, at least through a process of thought like that demonstrated in *On Moral Fiction*, seems to be the logical end product of the observable and sustained impulse that I started out in this essay by calling nostalgia. I believe that I can understand why it happens. It's true that the world of the present may be insufficiently satisfying or sustaining in a great number of ways, that it may no longer be able to create, simply by its own fecund and ongoing promise, a nourishing belief in the significance and certainty of the future, or even of the present. It's even possible that our age is unprecedented in the precise nature and extent of the mass humiliation, generalized paralysis, and withering terror and threat that it gives us, presenting all those on earth with the prospect of entire lifetimes trapped between "unremitting banality and inconceivable terror." Yet these still are inadequate reasons to respond to such prospects with willful blindness, to avoid the truth of the present world under the claim of putative or self-congratulatory higher values, or, above all, to ignore the truth of history and seek complacent or desperate escapes by any variety of means into the mythical comforts of a non-existent and falsely idealized past. More than this should be expected of serious writers of a serious literature, or for that matter of a general intellectual culture itself if it may be said still to be genuinely alive, or to hold out promise of any real or dignified hope for a future that, no matter what else may or may not happen, is destined to come.

Galway Kinnell

The Fundamental Project of Technology

"A flash! A white flash sparkled!"
  Tatsuichiro Akizuki, *Concentric Circles of Death*

Under glass, glass dishes which changed
in color; pieces of transformed beer bottles;
a household iron; bundles of wire become solid
lumps of iron; a pair of pliers; a ring of skull-
bone fused to the inside of a helmet; a pair of eyeglasses
taken off the eyes of an eyewitness, without glass,
which vanished, when a white flash sparkled.

An old man, possibly a soldier back then,
now reduced down to one who soon will die,
sucks at the cigarette dangling from his lips, peers
at the uniform, scorched, of some tiniest schoolboy,
sighs out bluish mists of his own ashes over
a pressed tin lunch box well crushed back then when
the word "future" first learned, in a white flash, to jerk tears.

On the bridge outside, in navy black, a group
of schoolchildren line up, hold it, grin at a flash-pop,
swoop in a flock across grass, see a stranger, cry,
hello! hello! hello! and soon, *goodbye! goodbye! goodbye!*
having pecked up the greetings that fell half unspoken
and the going-sayings that those who went the morning
it happened a white flash sparkled did not get to say.

If all a city's faces were to shrink back all at once
from their skulls, would a new sound come into existence,
audible above moans eaves extract from wind that smoothes
the grass on graves; or raspings heart's-blood greases still;
or wails babies trill born already skillful at the grandpa's rattle;
or infra-screams bitter-knowledge's speechlessness
memorized, at that white flash, inside closed-forever mouths?

To de-animalize human mentality, to purge it of obsolete
evolutionary characteristics, in particular death,
which foreknowledge terrorizes the contents of skulls with,
is the fundamental project of technology; however,
the mechanisms of *pseudologica fantastica* require,
to establish deathlessness it is necessary to eliminate
those who die; a task attempted, when a white flash
    sparkled.

Unlike the trees of home, which continually evaporate
along the skyline, the trees here have been enticed down
toward world-eternity. No one knows which gods they
    enshrine.
Does it matter? Awareness of ignorance is as devout
as knowledge of knowledge. Or more so. Even though not
    knowing,
sometimes we weep, from surplus of gratitude, even though
    knowing,
twice already on earth sparkled a flash, a white flash.

The children go away. By nature they do. And by memory:
in scorched uniforms, holding tiny crushed-metal lunch tins.
All the ecstasy-groans of each night call them back, satori
their ghostliness back into the ashes, in the momentary
    shrines,
the thankfulness of arms, from which they will go
again and again, until the day flashes and no one lives
to look back and say, a flash, a white flash sparkled.

William Dickey

Armageddon

I see it in terms of images: humans and angels.
An allegorical war with arms reaching out of clouds
their hands bristling with jagged cut-paper thunderbolts.
On the earth beneath dark women in dark red shawls
cower soliciting mercy, demonstrating their innocent babies.
The Lord, who is a father or the chief executive officer
of a celestial corporation, is displeased.

It will not be like this. I sat in the car one summer
during lunch breaks at the frozen foods plant, reading
   Hiroshima
when it first came out. The picture that is in my mind
is of people, vaporized by an unexpected sun
and only their shadows left burned into the wall behind them.
In their eyes it was the shock of noon forever.

I try to convince myself how that would be:
the lovers in their spacious bedroom with a wall of windows
open gratefully to the air; they are serene and affectionate,
their passion musically resolved; a hand stroking the relaxed
   dark hair.
Then all this struck into nothing, and a flat shadow
like a child's decoration on a funeral dish:
what remains forever to occupy the room.

Leonard Woolf said that there would be war
because the generals, having devised their weapons,
and seen them manufactured, the sleek expensive mechanisms,
would have to try them out, and it is true.
There is no invention of man that has not been used
if it was capable of being used, and these are.
Electric cattle prods defame the soft personal testicles.

But from this Armageddon, at the storm's center,
not even a cry, not even the houses burning.
Less than that, less than anything in the known world.

I asked a young man about twenty, my student, whether
the thought of this possibility was in his mind
and he said yes, even at a loud noise
in the street he would think: now it is happening.
He does not have, as I do, to form images
to imagine the happening: for him it is already there
like the underwear that he puts on in the morning.
It is with him all the time, as his shadow is.

"And he gathered them together into a place called in the
    Hebrew tongue Armageddon.
And the seventh angel poured out his vial into the air;
and there came a great voice out of the temple of heaven,
from the throne, saying, It is done."

The language deceives us, like the language of "peace with
    honor."
If it can be said so nobly, must it not be a noble thing?
So much language hoping to soothe us away from the fact
of death, death without ritual, the procession of ritual
    mourners
evaporated with him they would have mourned, no distinction.
No context to absorb and make valuable the loss.

The language of the previous verse is better:
"Behold, I come as a thief.
Blessed is he that watcheth, and keepeth his garments,
lest he walk naked, and they see his shame."

There are thieves among us, and they keep their garments.
They accumulate around them garments of steel.
They wait for their final garments of human shadow.
The lovers were naked, the air was calm, the sea
sparkled outside their final window. It was noon
when they became incident.

                    The mushroom cloud
ascending, the clock on the *Bulletin* cover
a minute from midnight. These images
we live under and among. The possibility of absence
so complete we will hardly have known what absence was.

Zoe Anglesey

Ragged Saturday

The day before the day of rest or the day
after a week's work, then desperate, wanting work
or the equivalent in pay, I go for chance money,
a lottery, luck, bingo, and not a bonus.
I collect coupons and notice the post office
draws to its wanted posters studious scrutiny.

Wretched with carbuncles, Marx devoted time explaining
how and why individuals, classes and countries sell
themselves. Can you imagine a black swallowtail
selling its gardens? Or the whales their oceans?
This makes me ponder, life fights degrees of ownership.
For the buyers, high finance gamblers play the game
putting on the board hands and baby teeth, whole valleys,
fins and wings, plantation crops and the magma core
of mountains, even cells and their microparts.

During coffee breaks through highrise windows,
wallstreeters see and dismiss another sort of gamble —
planted wheat living its term until combines comb
the harvest, a lesson below their noses — landfills
need design and a little throw away from the market.
No financiers. Yes, an artist, the midwife-farmer type,
dreamt up the wheat. She wanted to cure an urban bias.

This very ragged Saturday, wheat does not trickle.
It's too sad hungry in your own country.
How weird the need to bay, give life a chance,
trade rattling die for work. I'm telling you Vallejo,
you have Ministers of Health and Agriculture there.
You had Incan shamans and Paris. You believed faces
that looked back into your searching eyes.
Today screens and neon cataract for blindness.
Forests are cut and diamonds suffer the loss of light
in private vaults. Worse, we have fewer words to say.

William Zaranka

Blessing's Envoi

> to colonize the air
> with thoughts as swerveless
> as bombers.
>   — *Wayne Dodd*

When a book ends it is like doomsday.

Blessing looks down on the swerveless bombers,
below them the provender is apportioned
in the mineshafts, and the government officials
eat the fig leaves and fuck their secretaries.

Unless there's a sequel. Then the ICBMs arc
in reverse from Moscow to New York,
the blond, grainy heartlands sway with plenty,
four stocky horses cough up their snaffles and yawn.

Will he be put to death under his covers tonight,
spooned by his wife, a room away from his son,
his hobby's balsa sections, brads, and plastic cement
left to collect the downsift, downwind of the blast?

Or will he carry on and in the morning wake
and gargle, a survivor, maimed but determined,
healing among the storm cellar's dry milk
and canned fruits and vegetables, tapping code in his head,

drawing on his walls the hunted buffalo
with what, tomato sauce? the colorful fruit juices?
so cold and fresh in the morning, a life
not worth living would not contain them,

would not find Blessing so insistent, pesky,
wheedling to stay alive, calling his debts and favors,
offering his heart and kidneys, both brown eyes,
his cadaver to the sciences but not his soul,

and to the reader of his pages, words.

Denise Levertov

Watching *Dark Circle*

'This *is* hell, nor am I out of it'
Marlowe, *Dr. Faustus*

Men are willing to observe
the writhing, the bubbling flesh and
swift but protracted charring of bone
while the subject pigs, placed in cages designed for this,
don't pass out but continue to scream as they turn to cinder.
The Pentagon wants to know
something a child could tell it:
it hurts to burn, and even a match
can make you scream, pigs or people,
even the smallest common flame can kill you.
This plutonic calefaction is redundant.

Men are willing
to call the roasting of live pigs
a simulation of certain conditions. It is
not a simulation. The pigs (with their highrated intelligence,
their uncanny precognition of disaster) are real,
their agony real agony, the smell
is not archetypal breakfast nor ancient feasting
but a foul miasma irremoveable from the nostrils,
and the simulation of hell these men
have carefully set up
is hell itself,
                 and they in it, dead in their lives,
and what can redeem them? What can redeem them?

Dark Circle (1982) is a film produced by Chris Beaver, Judy Irving, and Ruth Landy of
the Independent Documentary Group.

Katharine Haake

The Meaning of Their Names

Constance had visions of nuclear holocaust. She'd had them all her life, really, ever since the Rosenbergs were killed and her mother said to her father, "Now thanks to them we could be burned alive." Constance, who was four then, had a dream in which the father ate his peas and no matter where she ran—into the closet, under the bed, up the stairs—it turned into a fireplace. The stairs just disappeared and she fell beneath the flames, trying to run falling under red. But now that Constance was grown up she knew that when the time came there'd be no time for running, and so she was doing her running beforehand —not away from but toward the danger zone, which she meant in her own way to defuse.

It was June and at five in the morning the Sacramento Greyhound bus depot was as crowded as it had been half the night before when Constance finished scrubbing out the ladies' room and went home to pack her personal belongings in the purple shopping bag she'd got free at Macy's, though she bought all her clothes at Woolworth's. Today for her trip she had chosen the thin blue flowered dress with pearl buttons, and the white sweater, and her lightest of pale blue slippers. Constance's eyes were blue too, also perpetually startled, but her face had a rare, reliable quality, just short of grave, that saved it. As she waited she hummed, she shifted her bag, she pressed against the polished glass of Gate 4—destination, Salt Lake City, Cheyenne, Washington, D.C. Already behind her the floor was streaked with boot and suitcase markings, and there were cigaret butts and candy and Dorito wrappers, and over in the corner, a soiled paper diaper. But what did all that matter now when Constance had her bus pass tucked into her billfold, her fifty twenty dollar bills pinned to the inside of her cool cotton slip, her packed purple shopping bag and her manila envelope thick with petitions for nuclear disarmament?

Still, if Constance had her purpose, she also had her memories, her sense of the familiar, what she valued more than anything but peace. Half her life this year she'd lived in Sacramento, the better part by far, during which she'd learned to find the freshest quart of milk, the cheapest grilled cheese sandwich, the reddest pair of go-aheads. In the Greyhound coffee shop the waitresses would serve her just half a cup of coffee—to keep it hot—without her asking. The man who put newspapers in the boxes left one for her at the ticket counter free. She was liked and she liked it, but a first strike was a first strike nonetheless, and Sacramento was a target.

In the same way, all those years before, between the day the Rosenbergs were killed and the Cuban Missile Crisis, Constance had been terrified of her mother. The woman had a way about her, maybe calculated, maybe not, as if her own personal terror, somehow transformed to spite, might alone be enough to call down the wrath of nations. If her mother said now the Russians will orbit a man in space, the Russians orbited a man in space; if her mother said now the Chinese will get the Bomb, the Chinese got the Bomb. Constance calculated lifespans, particularly hers, in terms of projected technological developments: how long before how many had the knowledge and capacity to blow the world up. Then the Cuban Missile Crisis changed her whole perspective: survival taught Constance the power of firmness. To her mother she said she preferred to be called Constance. "Connie you've been called since the day you were born," her mother said. "Connie you'll be called until you die." Constance bridled but kept the peace, until to keep it further she had to pack and leave. It hadn't been easy then and it wouldn't be easy now, but no one had called Constance Connie since.

The driver, when he started taking tickets, nodded to Constance and did not check her pass. Constance took the seat behind his, propped her feet up on her bag, folded her red hands neatly in her lap and watched the other passengers as they boarded, watching her. Her gaze was ingenuous, inviting, theirs guarded, for Constance was a small woman, boyish, hard and muscular, and with enormous blond braids coiled and coiled around her tiny head and the daintiest, whitest teeth. Pearls, Duane had called them, perfect shining pearls all in a perfect shining row. Constance closed her lips, still smiling. A girl in a tight E.T. t-shirt and green heels tripped as she got on. Constance smiled harder. The girl caught her balance, hurrying back. An older man, pot-bellied, slow, with a black cane and white cowboy hat, tipped his hat kindly but also moved back. The women with babies, the fat boys with books, they all had their preferred locations on the bus, and not any beside Constance who still kept on watching them with that startled expression she had no control over, for Constance had it planned out in her head.

At first she and her seatmate would talk about what people talk about—probably the other person's family or health or religious beliefs, or maybe just the weather, where they were going, things like that, it didn't matter. Because time would, as it does, go on and they would cross the valley, there would be foothills, and then the long climb into the mountains. Constance smiled, more to herself. There, when they got to the mountains, it would be so green and cool, with a carpet of needles and small yellow flowers, and though you wouldn't be able to smell it on the bus, that fresh pine scent, like the more expensive brands of disinfectant. Constance, who had never been to the mountains, had seen pictures and knew. A feeling of peace would come over the travelers. They'd smile across the aisle, introduce themselves and offer to share sandwiches or hold their neighbor's child—just the same as in Constance's dreams when she defused the last bomb in the world and there was a great party in a meadow full of flowers, and people dancing to the music of fiddles and flutes, and children trailing bright-colored balloons.

Yes that would be the perfect time, up in the mountains, to bring out her petitions and give one first to the person beside her, then to the front, to the back, to the other side. Maybe the driver would announce it, maybe he'd let her talk on his little microphone. And what she would say then, she would say about nuclear war—its pros and cons—in such a way that no one would refuse to sign, if anyone ever could. Already to herself she was counting up the signatures—one for every person on the bus. And if you multiplied that number by the number possible on each petition, and if each person took only one petition with that person to that person's destination for people there to sign...

The bus pulled suddenly down familiar streets and Constance caught her breath. There was the rosebush, heavy and red, which not three months before she'd worried frost might kill; there, the Orange Julius where sometimes she had orange juice. They turned left; they turned right; Constance pressed her forehead to the window. Behind this fence that spring she'd found a pond with lilies and a waterfall, three swans and fist-sized goldfish. It was a sweet early April dusk when she had wandered past, and heard the swans sing out in mating, and stopped to part the vines. Week after week she had returned, listening for the squawk of ducklings. Now she closed her eyes and turned the pond into a fireplace, flames spouting up where water pummeled down.

Leaving a place was not at all like arriving, the way sixteen years before Constance had arrived in Sacramento with nothing but her handbag and the memory of her mother stationed in front of the family t.v. set. "They should send them all to jail," her mother kept insisting, "—Communists, nigger-lovers, Berkeley free-speech jerks. What's this country coming to?" Constance didn't care so much about the country then; she cared that her mother would be turning on her next. "Your hair's a mess. You have no breasts," her mother often said. "And why, oh why do you stay home Friday nights?" Constance left on Friday night and arrived in Sacramento in the morning, so of course when Duane smiled and offered her work she thought it would be fine to sweep out the litter and scour the restrooms: it was a job, and she liked things to be clean.

She liked things as they turned out, all in all. She took a small apartment near the depot; she took to a routine of working days, wandering evenings; it was fine. Sacramento was fine. The mall had concrete fountains to cool her feet in during summer; Breuner's had animated windows at Christmas. Breuner's was nice, really, any time of year. Constance liked to go there and dream of matching bedroom sets, if only she could think what to do with all the drawers. Put things in them probably— string and picture postcards and her pay stubs and all those flowers she collected from the edges of gardens when they bloomed.

But then that was the way she had always been, Constance— delighted with small pleasures and with her strong likes and dis- likes, so much more pronounced than those of others, and also lacking any sense of irony, humor or proportion. Even as a girl she'd lacked the grace of compromise, become excited over trifles—red shoelaces, snow—and been as likely to feel dis- tressed if chunks of white came off with the shell of her hard- boiled egg as she was when the President was killed. She also read books backward from her very first primer, a notion which her mother hoped would pass, but it didn't. Constance's notions never passed, and the way she had of framing them kept her apart from all other children—except for a short time a girl named Jan.

Jan moved to town the February of Constance's eleventh year and from the back seat in the last row stared across the classroom, her green eyes clear and knowing, at Constance. Constance stared back. The teacher took her aside and explained, "Jan's back is curved like an 'S'." "Snake," Jan told Constance, who thought the other girl's red braids and queer slumped shoulders beautiful. So they started sharing ribbons, Jan and Constance, for their hair, and lunches out among the boulders at the far end of the playground. Behind them there round California hills humped into bleak sky; chipmunks scolded; wind tore at live oak, buckbrush, manzanita. Constance particularly liked the wind, which made her feel alive and intimate. She'd never felt that way before, with the craziest ideas and not at all timid. Once she asked Jan what she thought it would be like. "*I* think," Constance said, "there will be a hot blow to the forehead, and then..." Jan broke apart an Oreo and licked at the sugary icing. "If it comes to that," she said, "I'd just as soon be dead."

On the bus the seats weren't as comfortable as Constance had remembered from her other bus trip years before. Her feet didn't touch the floor and her head, which hit right in the center of the rest hump, was angled forward at an awkward tilt. After the first thirty miles her neck began to ache. She tried to shift without seeming to squirm; she sat straight upright and pretended she was watching a Greyhound pay t.v. It really was like that, with the green-tinted window for the screen and all the cars outside and the riders in them, and every half hour or so, another town, another station—except, of course, there wasn't any music or talking, and no real characters either. Things could get boring without music or characters, so Constance hummed and made up stories about all the people she saw and how they were almost killed in the nuclear holocaust, but then by God's grace at the last terrible minute war was averted and everyone was saved. Constance especially liked saving little babies and every truck driver who reminded her of Duane.

The true thing is, from the time Duane hired her to the time he noticed her playing Let's Make a Deal for a matching bedroom set during her single morning break, Constance thought about his smile which showed, beneath a waxed red mustache, two front teeth shifted one tooth over to the left. It was the strangest thing. She'd be sweeping out the lobby and see him talking to a ticket agent, and the way he was leaning over the other girl would make her feel something where she never had before — almost like bomb drills at school, only nice. Or he'd come up behind her and put his hand on her shoulder, and all her blood would rush down. Constance never knew what to say at those times; even later at home she'd still feel unnerved. "Duane winked at me today," she'd say. "Did I wink back? Why didn't I wink back?" Then she'd take her chicken pot pie from the oven, and as she waited for it to cool, uncoil and unbraid her hair and sometimes unbutton her blouse just one more button. "Do you think he'd like me better this way?" she'd say. But by morning, every morning, she'd have lost her nerve again and gone to work as neat and tidy as she'd always been before.

Only feelings are feelings, especially certain kinds, and so it was inevitable that Duane would come to her that day she was trying for a matching bedroom set and take her to the baggage room and lead her to a box back in the far corner with Oriental writing on it and a two-week-old received date, and then ask her what she thought the sounds were that were coming from it. Constance bent over the box and listened. Duane was standing behind her. The sounds were not quite peeps, not quite chirps, a little squawkish. Constance said, "I think it's ducks." Duane put his hand on her shoulder. Constance said, "Sometimes on Sunday I go to the park and feed the ducks stale bread. This sounds like baby ducks." Duane's hand moved. She started to undo the string; he started to undo her hair. It was cool in the baggage room, with the smell of leather and of Duane's cheap cologne. There were so many ducks inside the box, little yellow fluffs, Constance couldn't count them all. Instead, she found herself counting the fingers on Duane's hands which had come around at last and were searching for her buttons, down her front. Soon she wasn't counting anything at all.

In the mountains nothing happened, and in Reno nothing happened either except that Constance won five slot machine nickles and bought Wrigley's chewing gum to share with the person she sat with, as she was done waiting for someone to sit with her. Even so it was hard to decide. Again and again Constance wandered up the aisle, down the aisle, finally selecting a broad-shouldered woman in a green skirt and sweater and with a small t.v. on her lap.

"Ma'am?" Constance said. "Please, ma'am, do you want a piece of gum?"

The woman looked up, smiling, like her shoulders, broadly. She extended her hand. "I'm Lucette, from Montreal."

"Constance," Constance said, "on my way to Washington."

Lucette made a sound in her throat like "ahh." Constance sat down. A black man brushed her knee, heading toward the rear, and a girl in Levis stretched out across both seats opposite. Lucette made that sound again. Shy suddenly, Constance checked her envelope, crammed in the top of her purple shopping bag. Then a man in a navy undershirt and shiny black polyester slacks paused before them, staring down from above. A tic at the corner of his nose made his whole face jump, and he smelled of cheap aftershave and whiskey. Lucette nudged Constance.

"*That* kind of man," she said. "*That's* the kind of man you have to watch."

"Watch what?" Constance said.

"They beat their wives. They slap their children to sleep," Lucette said, fiddling with the knobs of her t.v.

For one hundred miles across the desert Lucette watched a ballgame while Constance tried to match the teams up with dark uniforms and light uniforms. Every once in awhile the man put his head over the back of her seat and, grinning, asked the score. Underneath his chin, along the contour of his jaw, a red and black tattoo twisted like a diamond-backed snake. When he talked, the snake moved. Constance wanted to make the snake be still, but her head was full of her mission of peace and all she could think about was how did a person begin: with everything turning into a fireplace, or with the hot blow to the forehead? Lucette had such a stern forehead, high and so indelicately lined Constance had to fight back an impulse to reach over and smoothe it out. What she would have given to fill this other woman and the man and the rest of them with peace! But without the right and true convincing words she could only wait for the ballgame to be over. It was a very long ballgame. It would go on forever. Midway through the sixth inning, the t.v. reception went out.

"Oh," Constance said. "Oh."

Lucette laughed. "What the hell. My team was losing."

The man's head appeared above them, the snake's tail wiggling excitedly, but Lucette said something that made it disappear again. Constance was nervously prying at the flap of her envelope, which had stuck with moisture. Lucette stowed the t.v. under the seat.

"Men," she muttered, "they're all the same. What's he been drinking, I wonder? What's that you have there?" she asked Constance, sitting up.

Constance got the envelope open and thrust a petition at her. Then there was a pause, longer than she had anticipated. In her head she kept formulating arguments: the birds will be blinded, water will burn, our children will not be like us.

"I'll sign," the man behind them said. "Just give me a pen. Sign what?"

Constance said nothing.

At last Lucette said, "Tell me about it. I'm a nurse. *I* volunteered for Vietnam."

"Didn't I say I'd sign?" the man said.

But Constance didn't hear him now, heard nothing but the sudden beating of her own heart. She couldn't breathe and there were colored specks at the edges of her vision. Lucette was saying it was time, past time. Constance was trying to count but had forgotten her numbers. What came after seven? It wasn't possible. Lucette had been *there*, at the other war. And since she had been there, she might have, could she have...

"Oh sure," Lucette said when Constance got her question out, "I knew hundreds of Duanes. Duane this, Duane that..."

Constance grabbed her arm. "No please, I have to know. Did this Duane have red hair — red hair and a waxed red mustache?"

"I knew a red-headed Duane," the man behind them said, then got up and went to the back for a smoke. Lucette looked away too, but not quickly enough that Constance didn't see the new look come into her eyes, with something sad about it, and tender, and made almost unbearable by what must have been an inconsolable loss. Constance waited — maybe one minute, maybe ten, she'd lost all sense of time. At last Lucette said that, well yes, he'd had red hair, he'd had blond hair, he'd had black hair — they'd all of them had hair if it wasn't burned off.

The baby ducks were all over the floor before Duane and Constance remembered them, and Constance ran around naked, laughing and scooping them up to lay in the cradle of Duane's cupped hands. They filled their pockets and kissed some more. Constance took home seven ducklings she made a place for in her bathtub and kept them there until one died. It was very sad. All one night she knelt on the cold tile floor, watching it in hopes it might get up, but the feathers were so damp and already there was a bad smell. Afterwards, because Duane said it was best, she let him put the others out of their misery. That was the only time he came to her apartment, and he was so cool and calculated, sitting on the porcelain edge of her tub and snapping, one by one between his fingers, the six remaining yellow necks. Constance cried and wished she'd thought to set them free in the park, but when Duane found out what was wrong, he said they weren't natural ducks anyway and would have died soon enough in that kind of wild environment. Constance felt something funny twist inside her when she heard the words *that kind of wild environment*, and she never could, no matter what, forget them.

But for three years, as long as Constance was with Duane, Constance didn't care, for though the way they were together was not like other people, neither was Constance, and so she was happy. Nothing could have pleased her more than that she and Duane should meet as they did in the baggage room for one thing and one thing only, the way they both preferred, simple, to the point and beyond the necessity of either thought or speech. She liked the musty smells too, and the dim light, and the cold hard feel of the luggage rack beneath her. Far away she could hear the people in the station; close, Duane's breathing and his heart. That was best. That, and that they'd dress when they were done and go their separate ways, knowing they'd be at it again before too long. That really was best — mute acquiescence, perfect agreement — for if the nature of solitude were deathly still and luminescent as a nimbus, Duane had let himself so cleanly into Constance's it was altered only insofar as it was made safe. Nothing, not even nuclear war could destroy this, what she had with Duane. How could there be nuclear war when there was this?

Lucette's hand was on Constance's shoulder, not shaking or squeezing but just resting there, more an acknowledgement than an apology. They sat like that for awhile, the two women, one large, one small, before either could find it in herself to

55

break the silence. Then it was Lucette who spoke, not at all shy to admit she dreamed of peace too. She gestured up and down the aisle with a broad, expansive sweep of her arm.

"We all do," she said, "every one of us on this bus. How could we not?"

But Constance was still upset. She frowned; she didn't know. "If all people dream of peace," she said, "why are things the way they are?"

"Ah that," Lucette said. "That's just the way it is. Why does that man have a snake beneath his chin?"

Constance frowned harder; the man seemed fine to her. She really was trying to understand.

"Well never mind then," Lucette said. "I may be right but I may be wrong. Let's ask the others and see what they say."

And by the time they reached Chicago, where their routes diverged, she and Constance had done just that, discovering in so doing what Lucette had said was true. For everyone along the way—including all the drivers and the girl in green heels and her new boyfriend and, before he got thrown out for drunkenness in Iowa, the tattooed man, who as he was leaving told Constance she had such pretty eyes and too good a heart for this world—had signed, and Constance had her hope and optimism back.

But it was somehow not the same. She didn't know. Either people signed right off, or they signed after thinking about it. In the end their motives were alike—for their own good. Constance wanted that their motives should be different. She wanted that they shouldn't have their weaknesses and prejudices, which showed so clearly in their eyes, in how they slung their bodies back against their seats. Where had they been when the other war was on? Why had they strayed so far from home? Constance, who knew about fear, couldn't hold theirs against them. But Constance had seen beyond her own and believed if they did too everything might suddenly be changed.

Only Constance was a small person, just like them, and such grace was not in her power. Grace of that magnitude lay alone in the power of the greater men and women to whom she would deliver her petitions. So she knew in her heart all she could tell the others, if she could tell them anything, was simply to go home, keep tidy kitchens and the peace, and let themselves be heard. However small they might be, they might, by living just and proper lives, transcend the limitations of their size and move the greater people to recognize the meaning of their names. Constance kept counting names. To her they appeared as the multitudes.

It wasn't nuclear war but the war in Vietnam Constance should have feared for herself years back, for when it reached a certain pitch, Duane enlisted. Nine months later he was dead. And what Constance felt then was not grief so much as betrayal, for there had been about their wanton encounters something that, while they were taking place, eased an unacknowledged emptiness inside her, and while they weren't, exacerbated it. But Constance had cared so little for introspection and the common realms of meaning in those days the terms seemed unimportant. All that seemed important was that she should be in the baggage room on time at the designated times. *That* had been her mistake, her only mistake, apparently small but in fact of such proportions it took Duane's untimely death to teach her what she'd really felt was love. Not even Constance's mother could have argued with that, but it changed everything. For in Constance's head now Duane took the only form she could imagine for him — husband. He had been husband and she had been wife.

Constance didn't know what to do with that, so at first she did what she'd always done — go to work, wander, dream of matching bedroom sets, feed ducks. But there were different laws in operation now and little by little Duane's world intruded. Constance tried thinking about it. She thought and thought. Eventually she thought to ask the man who put newspapers in the boxes for a copy and read it back to front, intensely interested, as she was when she was young, to get to the beginning and see how it all started. She thought about how it all started. And then she thought since Duane was killed in Vietnam she should demonstrate against the war, but Constance was terrified of crowds and rhetoric. She thought about writing the President, but what could she possibly say? At last she thought if she could somehow memorialize Duane's passing it would be as if he never passed at all. Order would be restored and Constance could return in her own life to the steadiness of purpose her perfect isolation had always in the past sustained for her.

So Constance started keeping casualty figures on blue and yellow notecards — blue for Americans, yellow for Vietnamese. The figures increased by alarming proportions. Constance bought more cards, and then more cards and more cards. It was frightening. She filled recipe files, shoeboxes and every empty drawer in her imaginary matching bedroom set. The war ended but she couldn't stop. She bought fat black felt pens and started keeping records on the walls of her apartment. Names lost significance. She resorted to numbers: 7,000 in Argentina; 45,000 in El Salvador; 80,000 in Lebanon; 2,000,000 in Cambodia. Constance thought about the number two million; she thought about the murder in the bus depot that fall. And she kept adding and adding: 2,000 in Northern Ireland; 5,000 in Turkey; 10,000 in Chile; 25,000 in Zimbabwe, in Ethiopia, in Guatemala; 50,000 in Nicaragua; 100,000 in Afghanistan; 2,000,000 in Nigeria. The deaths went on and on—ten million in all, all violent—so engaging Constance in the minutiae of recording and remembering that she forgot for almost a decade the other, greater danger. But that was not to be escaped and Constance knew it, and so with the resumption of the Cold War in the eighties she was not taken by surprise but rather, at last, inspired to action. For that kind of number was unimaginable. That kind of number was not to be written or fathomed. That kind of number sent her reeling— eventually off to Washington, D.C., armed with her petitions and her faith.

But Washington, when she arrived, was not what she expected. It was hot and crowded and noisy, and though so much was the same—the black plastic waiting chairs and gates with destinations and people traveling places—not at all like Sacramento, which suddenly Constance felt very far from. There, she had the confidence of habit; here, she felt crumpled and confused. Her ankles were swollen, her neck wouldn't turn without pain and all over she had an unclean feeling. Just if Constance could get clean, that would help, and maybe spend a moment to compose herself. Only where was the baggage room in Washington, where the clean and private washroom?

Constance stared disconsolately at her bag and envelope. No one cared very much about cleanliness in Washington. The lobby smelled of rancid hotdogs and if a Coke spilled on the floor the Coke stayed there, with people tracking Coke footprints all over and the sticky slap hiss of their shoes peeling off. They had so many different colored shoes, this huge, dark, steaming throng—darker than in Sacramento, black not brown, and much more crushed together. Bodies had no discreteness. Arms were as likely to wrap themselves around you as to shove you out of the path, faces to spit as to nuzzle at your neck, hips to knock you down as to rub you there. It was all one thing, flesh against flesh. Constance stumbled, grabbing for her envelope as her bag spilled out in front. The voice on the loud-speaker repeated you should watch your personal belongings. Constance watched hers scatter. If only, if only she could just sit down.

Constance didn't know how long it took, but somehow she made it to the far wall near the t.v.'s—chairs all occupied—where she found herself towering above a no-legged beggar on his platform. Instinctively she tried to give him a petition, but he cursed and pushed himself away without knowing what it was. Near tears, Constance hugged the envelope. She missed Lucette; she even missed the man with the snake beneath his chin. What kind of snake was it really, she wondered—a rattlesnake? a cobra? She shuddered. Someone was watching her; she could feel it. Then she saw him and was washed through with relief.

Not twenty feet away a nice-looking young man in a uniform was watching her with interest, and his t.v. wasn't on. Constance smiled, hoping he might offer her his seat. He didn't move, but his socks were so white and his blond hair cropped so close to his head and his cheeks so smooth and pink and covered with such soft down Constance wanted to touch it. She wanted suddenly to sit down in his lap and rest her head upon his shoulder. The last time she'd seen Duane he'd been wearing the same uniform. It was a fine uniform, khaki and neat. Constance smiled again, this time meeting his eyes. Then they couldn't look away. Beneath his white eyelashes green irises, flecked with gold, pulsed, making the dark pupils big, small. Constance's own eyes grew wider. They kept staring and staring at each other, until after awhile the boy—for he was really more that than a man—said something to a squat, black woman at his side, who shook her head and left. And Constance took her place.

So much she wanted to talk to the boy, to thank him, to tell him what she'd been through and why and ask his help, but she was so tired and the chair was so comfortable—familiar and curved just right for her body—that almost at once she started drifting off to sleep. The sounds of the station were reduced to a hum; all colors merged. Beside her she could feel the boy's eyes caress her, from her big blond braids to her pale blue slippers.

And then in that state, half awake, half asleep, terrifyingly, Constance heard the bells of game shows the way she heard the school bell long ago one February noon with Jan—three loud short rings, a pause; three loud short rings, another pause. Constance knew at that moment what her mother said was true, and she bent and put her arm across her forehead to shield it from the hot blow, calling helplessly out that they must go in, they must go in: *this could be a real war.* The young man at her side shifted nervously. But Jan was already hiding deep among scrub oak, laughing and calling back that she'd rather be dead, she'd rather be dead, she'd rather...

"I wasn't constant," Constance said. "We could have been burned alive, but she was my friend and I wasn't constant."

"Ma'am?" the young man said.

And that's what Constance had said years before, after, when they were safe, to the teacher, in front of everyone: *We could have been burned alive and Jan wasn't even scared. She's with them. She wasn't even scared.* The game show bells went right on ringing. In spite of herself Constance laughed out loud, but not like it was funny, for now she knew that's what Duane had meant.

"*That's* what he meant," she said.

"Ma'am?" the young man said again, and in his voice there was a queer edge too. "Who, ma'am?"

But Constance was thinking that a person was born to a certain world and that outside that world, in the wild environment, anything could happen. So yes it was Constance herself who had been Jan's wild environment, and Jan's back had curved and curved, and then Jan moved away. And Vietnam was Duane's, and Duane was dead. And Washington... Constance sat upright, awake at last, and looked around her. Maybe *this* was *her* wild environment. She had come so far with such great hopes, gathering the multitudes within her. But now they were without again, surrounding, closing in.

"Ma'am?" the young man said for the third time, and finally the odd voice broke through so that when Constance turned to him everything cleared. Once more she felt filled with love, for in his bland, almost featureless face she saw them all—Lucette and Jan and Duane and the man with the snake chin and the drivers and the rest. Constance had never known such serenity as this. Between them, her and the boy, whom she loved, they contained the multitudes. The boy stood. Constance did too, smiling, loving him so. Maybe all wouldn't go as well as she'd planned; maybe her petitions would have to wait until she found the right, the proper time and place to deliver them. But it would be all right. She could work here for awhile at the D.C. Greyhound station, scrubbing down, disinfecting. And as she did, she could collect more signatures, and more and more, starting now with the young man standing straight and tall before her.

Constance reached into her envelope. The boy took a step back. Constance grabbed his arm. The boy was shaking his head, but she wasn't looking at him. She was looking at the multitudes. To the multitudes she thrust a blank petition. The boy put up his hand. Constance opened her mouth to sing out then and there with the message of the multitudes, but just as her voice caught hold of the first, the most important word — peace — it choked it back again. For when the boy saw what she wanted, he didn't sign. He backed away.

Blaga Dimitrova

The Water Buffalo (Hanoi, 1972)

Translated by John Balaban and Vladimir Phillipov

The rain drizzled and shifted
over rippling green fields of rice.
Every drop will grow a grain.

The lop-eared banana leaves
opened an umbrella over me
and I sank into an ancient hush.

Blaga Dimitrova

An old man with a buffalo
stood at the end of the path.
Both were carved in wood.

Without a word the old man
parted a curtain of leaves
to let me into his house.

I stepped across the threshold
and froze before a gaping hole,
a crater bigger than a grave.

Smoke rose from ashes,
black smoke curling in the wind.
Dry wells, instead of walls.

My host slid down to the bottom,
calling me, with beckoning hand,
to his family in the pit.

His grandson—a tuft of hair,
His old woman—the handle of a pot,
His strapping sons—bloody stones.

His pretty girls—threads of cloth,
His sons-in-law—sandal thongs,
His daughters-in-law—lumps of earth.

His brother, on a visit—a broken stool,
His great grandson, still in the womb
of his mother—a banana shoot.

The shoot, as if still growing,
had a green bud which resembled
the clenched fist of a baby.

...To have lived a long life honestly,
to have raised a big family
by yourself, and in your old age

to be left alone with your buffalo,
the only living creature
with whom to share your sorrow.

The inventions of America, those
gadgets, machines, technical wonders —
is this what they are for?

Eugene Dubnov

While Up the Hradčani

Translated by the author and Chris Arkell

While up the Hradčani the heavy armour
Droned to the city that had been undone
That day, a woman groaned in final labour
And painfully gave birth to her first son.

The boy's first cry was lost beneath the clatters
Of military hobnails on the street
Where loaded rifles were deciding matters
For Senators accustomed to defeat.

The father was not waiting for his offspring;
The sun had clotted in Vltava's eyes;
And in the square Jan Palach was ascending
Jan Hus's fire and felt the flames arise.

And as you raise your arms above the squads
Crossing your child in prayer for life and joy —
Mother, what is the trial by fire that God's
Determined shall be suffered by your boy?

Robert Penn Warren

New Dawn

1 *Explosion: Sequence and Simultaneity*

Greenwich Time	11:16 P.M.	August 5	1945
New York Time	6:16 P.M.	*"*	*"*
Chicago Time	5:16 P.M.	*"*	*"*
San Francisco Time	3:16 P.M.	*"*	*"*
Pearl Harbor Time	1:16 P.M.	*"*	*"*
Tinian Island Time	9:16 A.M.	*"* 6	*"*
Hiroshima Time	8:16 A.M.	*"*	*"*

2 *Goodbye to Tinian*

Now that all the "unauthorized items" are cleared
   from the bomber, including
The optimistic irrelevence of six-packs
Of condoms and three pairs of
Pink silk panties. Now that
The closed briefing session of midnight
Is over, with no information from Colonel Tibbets,
   commander, on the
Secret, obsessive question of every crewman — What
Is the cargo? From Tibbets only
That it is "very powerful." Now that
The crew, at the end of the briefing,
Have taken what comfort they can from the prayer
Of their handsome chaplain, a man's man of
Rich baritone — "Almighty Father,
Who wilt hear the prayer of them that love Thee,
We pray Thee to be with those
Who brave the heights
Of Thy heaven..."

And now that around the bomber the klieg lights
Murdering darkness, the flashbulbs, the barking
Of cameramen, the anonymous faces preparing to be famous,
The nag of reporters, the handshakes, the jokes,
The manly embraces,
The scrape of city shoes on the tarmac,

The news
From weather scouts out that clouds hovering over
The doomed world will, at dawn,
Probably clear. And,

Now down to brass tacks, Lewis,
The flawless co-pilot,
Addresses the crew, "...just don't
Screw it up. Let's do this really great!"

3 Takeoff: Tinian Island

Colonel Tibbets, co-pilot beside him,
Lays hand to the controls of the plane, which he
Has named for his mother, Enola Gay.

Pocketed secretly in Tibbets's survival vest,
Under the pale-green coverall, is the
Metal container of twelve capsules of cyanide.
These for distribution to command
   if facing capture.

Though a heavy-calibre sidearm would serve.

The tow jeep strains at the leash. Wheels,
Under the weight of 150,000 pounds,
Overweight 15,000, crunch
Off the apron, bound for the runway. Position taken.

"This is Dimples Eighty-two to
North Tinian Tower. Ready for
Takeoff instructions."

So that is her name now. At least in code. Dimples.

"Tower to Dimples Eighty-two. Clear
To taxi. Take off on Runway A, for Able."

At 2:45 A.M., August 6, Tinian Time,
Tibbets to Lewis:
"Let's go!"

All throttles full forward,
She roars down the runway, flicking past
Avenues of fire trucks, ambulances, overload
The last gamble, and runway
Now spilling furiously toward
The black sea-embrace.

Who would not have trusted the glittering
  record of Tibbets?

But even Lewis cries out. Grabs at controls. Tibbets,
Gaze fixed, hears nothing. Time
seems to die. But
Iron hands, iron nerves tighten at last, and
The control is drawn authoritatively back. The carriage
Rises to show
The air-slick belly where death sleeps.

This at cliff-verge.

Below, white skeletal hands of foam
Grope up. Strain up.

Are empty.

4 Mystic Name

Some 600 miles north-northwest to Iwo Jima, where,
In case of defect developing in the "Enola Gay,"
Tibbets wil land, transfer cargo to
The waiting standby plane,
And take over. If not necessary,
No landing, but he will rendezvous
With weather planes and the two B-29s
To fly with him as observers.

At 3 A.M., well short of Iwo Jima, code lingo
To Tinian Tower: "Judge going to work" —
Innocently to announce the arming
Of the cargo. The cargo,
Inert as a sawed-off tree trunk ten feet long,

Over two feet in diameter, five tons in weight, lies
In its dark covert.

It is
So quiet, so gentle as it rocks
In its dark cradle, its namelessness. But some
Name it "The Beast," and some,
With what irony, "Little Boy." Meanwhile,
It sleeps, with its secret name
And nature.

Like the dumb length of tree trunk, but literally
A great rifle barrel packed with uranium,
Two sections— forward one large, to rear one small, the two
Divided by a "tamper" of neutron-resistant alloy.
All harmless until, backed by vulgar explosive, the small will
Crash through to
The large mass
To wake it from its timeless drowse. And that
Will be that. Whatever
That may be.

5 *When?*

When can that be known? Only after
The delicate and scrupulous fingers of "Judge"
Have done their work. After
   1. Plugs, identified by the color green,
      Are installed in waiting sockets
   2. Rear plate is removed
   3. Armor plate is removed
   4. Breech wrench frees breech plug
   5. Breech plug is placed on rubber mat
   6. Explosive charge is inserted,
      Four units, red ends to breech
   7. Breech plug is reinserted, tightened home
   8. Firing line is connected
   9. Armor plate is reinstalled
  10. Rear plate is reinstalled
  11. Tools are removed
  12. Catwalk is secured

Robert Penn Warren

In that dark cramp of tunnel, the precise
Little flashlight beam
Finicks, fastidious, over all.

Soft feet withdraw.

Later, 6:30 A.M., Japanese Time, last lap to target, green
    plugs
On the log, with loving care, tenderly, quietly
As a thief, will be replaced by plugs marked
Lethally red.

6 *Iwo Jima*

Over Iwo Jima, the moon, now westering, sinks in faint
    glimmer
Of horizon clouds. Soon
The heartbreaking incandescence of tropic dawn,
In which the "Enola Gay" loiters for contact
With weather scouts and two B-29s,
Which rise to attend her: observers.

Weather reports good from spotters.
Three options: Nagasaki, Kokura, Hiroshima.

But message of one spotter:
"Advise bombing primary"— i.e.,
Hiroshima.

Already preferred by Tibbets.
What added satisfaction it would have been to know that
At 7:31 A.M., Japanese Time, the all-clear
Signal sounds over Hiroshima.

7 *Self and Non-self*

Tibbets looks down, sees
The slow, gray coiling of clouds, which are,
Beyond words, the image
Of sleep just as consciousness goes. He looks up, sees

Stars still glaring white down into
All the purity of emptiness. For an instant,
He shuts his eyes.

Shut your own
Eyes, and in timelessness you are
Alone with yourself. You are
Not certain of identity.
Has the non-self lived forever?

Tibbets jerks his eyes open. There
is the world.

8 Dawn

Full dawn comes. Movement begins
In the city below. People
May even copulate. Pray. Eat. The sun
Offers its circular flame, incomparable,
Worship worthy.

9 The Approach

Speed 200 miles per hour, altitude
31,060 feet, directly toward the
Target control point of Aioi Bridge. On time. On
Calculation. Polaroid glasses
(Against brilliance of expected explosion)
Ordered on. Color
Of the world changes. It
Changes like a dream.

10 What That Is

What clouds remain part now, magically,
And there visible, sprawling supine, unfended,
    the city.
The city opens itself, offers itself,
As in breathless expectancy.

Crossed hairs of bombsight approach
Aioi Bridge, as specified, on time,
For the target. Ferebee, bombadier, presses
Forehead devoutly to the cushion of bombsight.
Says, "I've got it."

The bomb is activated,
Self-controlled for the six-mile earthward
Plunge, and at that instant the plane,
Purged of its burden, leaps upward,
As though in joy, and the bomb
Will reach the calculated optimum of distance
Aboveground, 1,890
Feet, the altitude determined
By the bomb's own delicate brain.

There,
The apocalyptic blaze of

New dawn

Bursts.

Temperatures at heart of fireball:
50,000,000 degrees centigrade.

Hiroshima Time: 8:16 A.M., August 6, 1945.

11 *Like Lead*

Of that brilliance beyond brilliance, Tibbets
Was later to report a taste "like lead."

12 *Manic Atmosphere*

Now, after the brilliance,
Suddenly, blindly, the plane
Heaves, is tossed
Like a dry leaf in
The massive and manic convulsion of
Atmosphere, which, compressed, from
Earth, miles down,

Bounces.

The plane recovers.

Again, then, the heave, the tossing.

With recovery.

13 *Triumphal Beauty*

Now, far behind, from the center of
The immense, purple-streaked, dark mushroom that,
   there, towers
To obscure whatever lies below,
A plume, positive but delicate as a dream,
Of pure whiteness, unmoved by breath
   of any wind,
Mounts.

Above the dark mushroom,
It grows high— high, higher—
In its own triumphal beauty.

14 *Home*

Later, home. Tinian is a man's only home—
The brotherly hug, the bear-embrace,
the glory, and
"We made it!"

Then music, then solemn
Silence of the pinning of the medal,
The mutual salute. At last,
The gorging of the gorgeous feast
To the point of vomit, the slosh
Of expensive alcohol
In bellies expensively swollen.

15 *Sleep*

Some men, no doubt, will, before sleep, consider
One thought: I am alone. But some,
In the mercy of God, or booze, do not
Long stare at the dark ceiling.

Sharon Olds

When

I wonder now only when it will happen,
when the young mother will hear the
noise like somebody's pressure cooker
down the block, going off. She'll go out in the yard,
holding her small daughter in her arms,
and there, above the end of the street, in the
air above the line of the trees,
she will see it rising, lifting up
over our horizon, the upper rim of the
gold ball, large as a giant
planet starting to lift up over ours.
She will stand there in the yard holding her daughter,
looking at it rise and glow and blossom and rise,
and the child will open her arms to it,
it will look so beautiful.

Aaron Kramer

Swan Song

Winter half gone and the first snow boded;
trains bulging with batteners down —
still on the lake in squads ungoaded
waft the swans amid younglings brown.

If through smoke-smutted panes we study
faces of birds, can we guess what they feel? —
clouds aimed grim against beak and body,
arctics born between them and their meal.

Let one lift, and the rest will follow —
yes, but which has the brains to lift?
"Bird-brain..." Fah! — not one is a swallow
blessed with the Capistrano gift.

Are they societies of poets
riding one last roll of calm?
transmigrated, the souls of stoics
teaching their chicks contempt for harm?

Winter half gone and the first snow boded;
trains bulging with batteners down —
still on the lake in squads ungoaded
waft the swans amid younglings brown.

Hiroshima: a 37-Year Failure to Respond

1.

On August 6, 1982 one of New York City's more enterprising television reporters expanded his coverage of the annual Hiroshima commemorations to include a couple of brief Chinatown interviews. When one resident responded frankly that Japan's brutalities against China had damaged his ability to pity the victims of the first atomic blast, a shockwave went off in my head.

Hearing my old hardheartedness of 1945 expressed publicly by another did not lighten the sense of guilt, but it did redefine my inability to feel, as I knew a decent man should feel, when the tidings of horror came. Not that I endorsed the bombing — far from it. I recall a pure and lasting hatred for "trigger-finger Truman," a revulsion at the official excuses given, "friendships" terminated when shopmates and neighbors praised the instant deaths of 100,000 "Japs" as preferable to the continuing deaths of U.S. servicemen. But there was no pure impulse toward mourning; and I — whose verse had been characterized by some critics as overly elegiac — uttered no lamentation for those crucified at Hiroshima and Nagasaki.

Small wonder considering the decade just ended. The explosion of an Ethiopian village under him had been described by Mussolini's pilot-son as "The quintessence of beauty"; that, and the attacks on Spain's open cities such as holy Guernica, the destruction of Rotterdam, the Baedeker assaults on Canterbury, Coventry, London, finally turned the skies over Germany into a retributive agent for my five bombardier friends who never came back, for me too in my blood and poems:

> Looking back, and being alone,
> I talked to the thunderbirds almost as though they were
>   mine.
> I said: "Grow impatiently, children; and when you are
>   grown
> we will teach you to make of your shadow a terrible
>   thing,
> to answer for Guernica deep in the nests of the Rhine,
> and carry the hopes of the nations high on your wing!"
>   "Night Shift, Detroit"

This is what raged in my heart when news came of the first atomic explosion, and this is what kept me from responding to that colossal, mind-blowing event in other than broad philosophic terms. "On the Harnessing of Atomic Energy" may not be good poetry, but it is of some historic interest as among the first published on the subject. Here are several stanzas:

> Rise from the altar, stand untied!
> drink deep, besot yourselves with power,
> and cry, cry out the chant of pride!
> Here is your high, triumphant hour.
>
> . . . .
>
> What shall they reach for next, the fingers?
> Our planet's fragile now, take care!
> Perhaps they'll harvest the sky, and fling us
> a crown of radiant stars to wear . . .

Unfist the sun! I hear a flower
weeping in thirst. Oh let your pride
listen! let not your highest hour
be called the time when blossoms died!

Two like-minded older poets produced sonnets of revulsion and warning at this time. In "God's Fire" William Rose Benét recalled Lowell's Civil War poem, "The Washers of the Shroud":

[He] never dreamed what power might be unlocked:
Raging inferno, consuming lava pit,
Fury of flame, with life's foundations split
Whether it change the world or God be mocked.
Time was, Time is! How fatefully the sound
Time shall be! tolls. Prometheus is unbound.

Percy MacKaye laid out even more plainly the choices before "Aquaterraerial Man":

... who shall build
Sublime self-images of beauty, or blast
The organism of his origins to yield
Star dust, for snuff of sniffing comets. Not
His armories, armadas, syntheses
Of chemic analyses, deflecting his thought
From solar wisdom in atom force — not these
Powers can empower him toward his spirit goal,
But only the self-purgation of his soul.

Indirect and generalized as our response was, it should be considered in terms of the prevailing "liberal" mood. On August 7th, under its exultant Hiroshima headline, the *New York Times* carried a prominent secondary item: 'BY GOD'S MERCY' WE BEAT NAZIS TO BOMB, CHURCHILL SAYS. A gargantuan headline blazed across page one on the 13th: ALLIES TO LOOSE MIGHTY BLOWS ON JAPAN IF SURRENDER IS NOT MADE BY NOON TODAY. The sub-headline declared: U.S. IRKED BY DELAY. That day's lead editorial roared: "... the United Nations stand ready to continue the war with increased fury until the ruins of Japan surpass those of Germany."

Turbulent years followed: cold war, Korean war, paranoia, hysteria, repression, and the persistent thud of atomic testing. The sense of Hiroshima entered my books almost at once, though never directly:

> Flower, factory, face — all high, unhurt.
> What fierce armada flew? what mutilation
> reached down invisibly, ripped us apart,
> that bells now bathe our wound in celebration?
> "Victory Comes to the Unbombed Cities"

In "The Tinderbox," a retelling of Andersen's story, war is depicted not in fairy-tale or even traditional pre-atomic terms, but as cataclysm. The smell of disaster sharpened dramatically in the pre-Vietnam period — but still there is not a single frank confrontation. A party-goer in Pompeii is imagined:

> ...Right now the southern sky
> sickly glowed; one almost could imagine
> the suburbs blazing. Blazing? A wild idea!
> There flew no hullabaloo of fire-engines...
> Could earth and sky be threatening to explode
> in one another's face? No, nothing more
> than the air-conditioner. His head cleared. He
> remembered that the next five Saturday evenings
> were lined up solid...And once the blinds were firmly
> drawn,
> no matter how it tried, the sky's sick glow
> couldn't get through, couldn't get through to the smile.

Perhaps the fact that at this moment my poems were being featured almost weekly in the *Village Voice* encouraged me to examine, in "Pompeii" and half a dozen other *Voice* poems, without actually spelling it out, the prospect of planetary annihilation. In "But Suddenly" I conjecture what sorts of activities "you" might be engaged in when you hear "WE INTERRUPT THIS PROGRAM..." "A Wind in the Courtyard" faces the new tenuousness of human life in terms of a wind that makes "remarks / about the half-built apartment-house down the block / with such a spacious lobby..." In "The Ledge," a rain-emptied street becomes emblematic of the looming holocaust:

In this total desolation
the changing of a traffic light
becomes a tremendous event
to which, like an earth unpeopled,
the rain-hit ledge responds...
milleniums click past,
perfectly timed, with no witness!...
Into my dream the rain
drones without melody or mercy:
"There'll be no more dangling of legs,
hair played with, voices twining;
only the traffic light changing!"

"And I Looked, and, Behold, a Whirlwind" takes its title from Ezekiel; like his, the prophecy is urgent, shrill. While inconceivable bombs pass their tests and "winds, at eighty miles an hour, / carry death across the Atlantic," Americans with no brains but money enough, "like chubby moles...are digging" private bomb-shelters!

Ah, poet: on behalf
of the bridge, so delicately poised,
on behalf of the trees
— like virgins fearing attack —
on behalf of the buildings
filled with precious footsteps,
on behalf of the one child in a hundred
who might some day read your poem
and the other ninety-nine who are that poem —

turn your ears to the wind of death,
your eyes to the derricks of death!
shout BEWARE! BEWARE! as if Ezekiel
stood again on his street-corner in Jerusalem...

2.

Poe's "Philosophy of Composition" seems to be, and on the surface is, no more than an exploration of his strategies in creating "The Raven." But Poe had in fact chosen that poem and the way it took shape as a symbol of the point he meant to demonstrate: namely, that *craft* rather than some nebulous Muse is the instrument by which a successful poem is made.

In the same way I am exploring my own *non*-creation of a poem on the nuclear theme as a possible symbol of the wide failure among poets on this most tremendous of subjects, perhaps parallelling other silences throughout the history of literature. In Russian poetry, for example, silence has long been considered a prophetic gesture. In American poetry from 1835 to 1900 (my focus in *The Prophetic Tradition in American Poetry*), I had to confront a vast variety of silences by those who considered themselves the most ethically alert poets of the time, some of whom filled their diaries, letters, and editorials with denunciation of national iniquity — from the Mexican to the Spanish-American War, from Osceola to Sitting Bull, from the mobbing of abolitionists to the burning of Catholic churches — yet kept their poetry free of all such issues.

In my case, certainly, it cannot be said that I have eschewed the nuclear issue out of fear that, in Emerson's words:

> If I refuse
> My study for their politique...
> The angry Muse
> Puts confusion in my brain.

Nor have I been as concerned as James Russell Lowell is about "striving Parnassus to climb / With a whole bale of *isms* tied together with rhyme." It seems to me that among Lowell's most memorable poems are those in which he makes "a drum of the shell" and succeeds in erasing "the distinction 'twixt singing and preaching" much as Jeremiah and Isaiah did.

For five years I devoted my craft to the anti-McCarthy resistance; for eight years I did the same in opposition to the Vietnam War. The poems of those long periods were hardly escapes from the nuclear theme; but McCarthy and Ladybird and Nixon were frankly easier to deal with. Defiance and wrath, let us admit, can be more comfortably expressed than terror. For thirty-seven years the shadow of catastrophe has crouched in my skull day and night — the way sex and death crouched in every Victorian skull until Whitman, a poet of heroic dimensions, dared to wrestle them into his verses.

Perhaps the long and short of it has been that I am not a Whitman, that I lack the heroic element necessary to pull the great dread out of my skull and deal with it in the colossal terms it requires. Allen Ginsberg was right to make *his* nuclear statement grandly, Whitmanesquely, and I was proud to publish his "Plutonian Ode" in the first volume of *West Hills Review: a Whitman Journal*. Who knows? Maybe one day I'll let myself go off on a Ginsberg "high" and out it will come — audience or no audience — the full lyric orgasm at last, the desperate love song to my planet.

My own worst nuclear statements so far seem to have been the most blatant ones, all in the form of "jingling" ballads born of a craving to "reach."

> Every hour upon the hour
> you are in the newsroom's power.
> No more cooing, no more kissing:
> like a crazy pair you listen...
>
> Can you hope for gloomier tidings?
> It will come. The twilight widens.
> On his courser's flank, disaster
> cracks the whip and cries out: Faster!...
> "They Who Wait"

On the other hand I concluded a group of children's poems with a ballad that, in its low-keyed, affirmative, utterly apolitical tone, transmitted a genuine sense of how much is at stake:

> If I had a hundred planets to choose from,
> the one I'd pick is the Earth.
> Some may have more light and less shadow,
> but lacking the colors of ocean and meadow,
> what is a planet worth?
>
> I love the silver bellies of minnows,
> the golden crusts of pies;
> I love the twilight's lavender banner,
> October's leaves growing slowly tanner,
> my sister's hazel eyes.
> "A Hundred Planets"

In the '70's I occasionally returned to the Hiroshima mood, with a revulsion tindered by and expressed through Vietnam:

Aaron Kramer

> ...by night,
> driving past your television screens,
> I come into a storm of gypsy moths —
> a white death —
> a snow of teeth
> against the lawns you dote on
> more than other people's children.
> Then I remember Egypt
> and am glad.
> Justice on high! hallelujah!
> the first of many plagues.
>
> "Gypsy Moths in the Suburbs"

> I set down this, a witness' report:
> when neighbors met, they talked of rain, of sport...
> But this is not to say that unconcerned
> they saw the fragile spires our champions burned;
> perhaps, like me, they felt within their stomachs
> a welling nausea, in their hearts hot shame;
> perhaps, while lullabied in August hammocks,
> they begged the sky for Sodom's hail and flame.
>
> "Considering My Country"

In "Forebodings" the theme is *almost* stated outright, as "all the world's trees" on a windy night "raise their voices / in one sustained primeval note":

> ...I imagine them
> in a time that is coming
> roused to such outcry, such lamentation,
> joined by the voice of neither beast nor man,
> heard neither by devil nor god.

But the most effective focus remained the falling of a sudden shadow on a simple human activity. It had happened in Covent Garden one night during Prokofiev's *Romeo and Juliet*:

> that instant when I'd gathered in the whole
> audience, like a grandfather observing
> cherubic skaters on a lake who laugh
> as if the blood will never turn to ice,
> as if the ice will never turn to blood.
>
> "Gilbert and Sullivan Night at the Proms"

80

It had happened many years earlier in crawling traffic outside
of Cleveland's ballpark:

> A fury seized all eyes, all lungs;
> ten thousand fists were shaking —
> as if they'd been plundered while asleep
> and now at last were waking.
>
> A glory swept them; all arose;
> with sparks the dust was showered —
> as if the plunderer of their bliss
> at last were overpowered.
>
> By the time we tore loose from the traffic snarl
> another inning had ended,
> and over their lives, while they watched the score,
> the darkness of doom descended.
>
> "Baseball Game"

By extraordinary coincidence my poetry returned to that very
baseball arena — where, on August 9, 1981, the whole country
tuned in to the All-Star Game and beheld thousands of hands
on chests at the opening anthem as the flag waved. That very
morning Reagan had announced his decision to go ahead with
the neutron bomb. It was the anniversary of Nagasaki. As an
accompanying note explains, I chose the Asian sonnet form to
commemorate that bombing.

ALL-STAR NEUTRON DAY: AUG. 9, 1981

The mouths of Auschwitz's unholy pillars
sent sacrificial incense toward the skies.
Now men ask: From the womb of Bachs and Schillers
how could there be a leaping forth of killers
without one gasp, one turning down of eyes?

At 7:30, just as we were drinking
our orange juice, the pillar of the land
that was the womb of Whitman and Abe Lincoln
sent from his mouth a smoke. Men will be thinking:
With gasp, with lowered eyes, did no one stand?

Here's how it was: twelve hours went past: the smoke
had settled in all lungs; we settled too
and switched our tubes on; pandemonium broke
in Cleveland's ballpark — red and white and blue.

As the anti-nuke movement gathered head, I attempted the
ballad form again — and was even less successful:

Every night, as your head snuggles down into bed,
with a smile you consider your children:
darling Joan, dearest Fred, what they did, what they
    said.
— But for them every night grows bewildering:
Is it love — to be fed, given doll, given sled,
while the monster's let in that may kill them?

Is it love — that you scream for a favorite team,
carry on about crabgrass — but cannot
give a thought to the theme of a megaton flame
more than mighty enough to melt granite?
Is it love — that you dream of your grandchildren's fame
while betraying your grandchildren's planet?

A particular moment — its loveliness, its transitoriness — may
finally be the best I can transmit, as it is the most precious and
vulnerable of targets. In "The 24th" I describe an astonishingly
warm day in late November enjoyed by the strollers in Port
Jefferson:

Such lifted faces!
seeds of care, of course,
under every smile, even the youngest,
but for a moment at least
the whole species gifted
with a sweetness lingeringly offered,
lingeringly savored,
as if this were humanity's last mild day
not for the year but forever.

Something similar occurred during Alfred University's summer
music series, directed by Joseph Fuchs. A number of Japanese
students performed that August night, and a violinist from

Mainland China, surreptitiously self-taught throughout the "cultural revolution," made her brilliant debut. I tried to record in prose how "the final number, a luscious Mendelssohn quartet," affected me:

At first I was enthralled by the music and the music-making; but midway through the work — perhaps due to the poignancy of the passage — other thoughts and feelings took command. The way the four earnest children sat there — leaning into their instruments, into Mendelssohn, into each other — and the way the rest of us, even our hitherto impervious computer-expert from California, sat leaning into the event — struck me as unbearably lovely, ineffable, fragile. Unable to clutch it, to keep it from ebbing, I found myself clutching the arms of the chair.

Four nights ago, in this very building high over the campus, 36 of us, the newly arrived "elder group," had been invited to declare for one another briefly who and what we were. Now we were on the verge of scattering — to our mortgages, our illnesses (the man in the second row, we now knew, had been refused a triple heart-bypass as "useless" some months back), our scalded lawns, our tolerant children, another hostel.

The four players seemed to be clutching their instruments as well. Five hours a day of practising together — then, after some weeks, a return to doting or deflating families all over the world...possibly to exchange Christmas cards or phone calls, possibly to vie for the same position with an orchestra — but never again to be hugged into one soul in this valley.

Mendelssohn could not have been sobbing for this particular valley: holy ground a thousand years to the tribe whose remnants wept perhaps from behind a rock or tree as their Mother Earth lay raped under plough and derrick. And the town of Alfred, its university, so sure of themselves now, how long will *their* hold last? Will a snow or something bigger follow one of these summers and stay too long, too deep? longer, deeper than the legendary May snows of '74?

My thoughts now outdistanced the music in desperation. I thrashed about for *something* that could indeed be counted on to endure: the students of these students, into whose nerves and fingers would flow the method of Joseph Fuchs?

the grandchildren of our grandchildren, who would lean into an event such as this in some valley, on some planet?

Nothing was guaranteed. Without difficulty I could imagine a universe shorn of Mendelssohn, of fingers, of ears. After all, hadn't Germany without a murmur swept away his name and his music — even the wedding march — for a dozen years, first in his homeland, then Austria, Czechoslovakia, Poland, France, and "Morgen die ganze Welt!" Had things gone differently? Hadn't China swept away *all* traces of *all* Western music without a murmur, also for a dozen years? Hadn't Hiroshima's sense of touch, of hearing, along with all its other senses, been wiped out in one split-second by just one baby-bomb? So I clutched the arms of the chair, clutched harder, as the last movement flowed inexorably to its last bars.

"U.S. Open: Sept. 12, 1982," a second prose-piece, allows another such event to ferment in my innards:

Sunday. The final Sunday. Late afternoon in Flushing Meadow. Already Lendl's losing frown is in shadow. Twenty thousand heads — a record — turn like clockwork — left right left right — through the long volley. Then a roar as Connors crushes him one more time. And still the match goes on, not one seat empty, thousands in the aisles; alert, well-groomed, they turn their heads left right left right, sophisticated, not one nuance lost, hearts tied to Jimmy Connors' racquet.

I think of all the empty seats the night my college held its first (and last) symposium on nuclear energy. Scientists only, on the podium — except for me — and not one English, fine arts, social science major in the crowd. It was the anniversary — the very hour — of Karen Silkwood's final ride. I polled the knowledgeable crowd — not ten had heard her name. I asked the empty seats where all the "culture people" were. Who would defend the future of *King Lear*, Beethoven's *Ninth*, the waterlilies of Monet? Didn't they have grandchildren in their loins, if not in Jersey? Should only chemistry professors and their pupils be concerned? Should only high-class jargon diagrams flash on the screen, and not my Nora's, my Joanna's smile as well? That night on Paumanok I read some passages of Whitman, praise for a flowering Long Island — 1855 — pre-Shoreham — every line a banner, a rebuke.

June 12 (and still left right left right go twenty thousand heads — the sun is setting): Setting out from Patchogue with the South Country Peace Group — expecting what? had been a burnt-out rebel all week long: going through the necessary motions, making connections, even stirred awake at 2 a.m. by new stanzas for an old anti-nuke ballad. But I'd approached the big day exhausted, wondering whether I could manage the train-ride let alone the march. Was it just a case of physical decay — or decay of the fighting spirit? There was no question of my being in it — only of what it would all amount to in the end.

Mid-Manhattan, the tremendous transfusion burnt-out rebels need: inching east on 42 St., eyes and blood devouring the faces and flotillas surging west in all their clean young passion; inching north past the reviewing stand, the speakers, trying not to notice that the multitudes — from Anchorage to Minneapolis, Japan to Norway, and especially Vermont, Vermont, Vermont, unheard-of villages — were mostly cheering one another, that the city was *not* out in force, not lining sidewalks, not (with few exceptions) even at the window. Finding my sign at last: SHAKESPEARE AGAINST NUKES: TO BE OR NOT TO BE!! and behind it marching the whole way, then way up and into Central Park alongside brother poet Raymond Patterson. On 44th and Broadway a woman shoves through, fiftyish, spitting obscenities at us for inconveniencing her crossing over...Monday: three big buttons on my lapel still — back in Patchogue for a swim at the "Y" — blank faces when I mention the Great March; one gent remarking what a shame to let the traffic be blocked off for hours, to make so many cops work on a weekend.

Sunset. The lights go on at Flushing Meadow. Lendl keeps losing, losing. Twenty thousand roar. Suddenly I stop despising them. Suddenly they, and Flushing Meadow, Lendl and Connors, grow excruciatingly beautiful on my bright new Zenith screen. Suddenly they become my roar, my placard — whether or not those knowledgeable left-righting heads have room yet for a losing, for a sunset more enormous than a thousand Hiroshimas — I at least am still alive...there must be *some* good reason; up I creak from the recliner, the burn-out, leave entranced poor Lendl and the rest, face the typewriter, the page at last, take a deep breath, deepest in years, return the volley.

Months pass; the energies expended on June 12th are not lost; election day referenda around the country confirm a newly crystallizing resistance. But the wheels of anti-diplomacy grind on in Washington, and Reagan neatly pins his "Moscow" label on the anti-nuclear movement. Meanwhile a letter from the *New England Review* arrives: I am invited to join other poets in speaking out on its pages. Yes, of course! (But to what end?)

Suddenly December 9th comes — a crazy day that haunts me into words perhaps not healthy to set down:

Already across America the name NORMAN MAIER recedes into a library News Index listing. Already I feel it fading, though only thirty hours have passed since he was granted, not the national dialog he demanded, but the dialog one expects from our police in such cases — a bullet in the brain.

The anti-nuke groups he tried to nudge, first in Miami, then in Washington, liked the old coot but disapproved his methods. I also disapprove. A threat to blow up the Monument — the nation's Number One Phallus? What could that accomplish but confirm Archie Bunker's view of anti-nukists as bomb-toting cartoon-loons? Segretti staged nothing better in the old days, when Nixon needed to turn heads as Reagan needs to now.

Yes, I disapprove. But I like the old coot; the police photo of him in '57 reminds me of me five years from now. I am touched by the helmeted presence of him pacing before lenses and gun-mouths, having found an E.T. sort of way for his slogan to be central at last (not fifty poets choiring each other in a quarterly as in a tree), still lone but now surrounded, hearkened to, bargained with, no longer pacing caged inside his life's failed walls but on the loose, alive, more so than millions in their spaced-out teens, the planet's heirs! — alive, forcing the President, the very Reagan, to scoop up his papers in a jiffy and play White House in a back room!

But need it be said? What is called for is not the blowing up of a harmless tower. We are the celebrators of towers, as of flowers.

Our voices may be small, but frustration must not be allowed to distort or mute them. A few days after the Great March I drove into Manhattan. The heavens over my beloved skyline were as bleak now as they had been radiant on the 12th. How else could the sign be read?

NEW YORK SKYLINE IN CLOUD

On other days
each prince of them
has seemed to raise
his diadem
in pride and scorn
against the sky
beyond the praise
of beings born
to burrow down
and kiss the hem
of his steel gown
and burst and die.

Now one and all
beneath the cloud
they seem less proud
nor half so tall
stripped bare and set
against a wall
with no alas
the faint hope lost
the lethal gas
about to jet
the Holocaust
about to fall.

Kolyo Sevov

An Afternoon's Wandering

Translated by John Balaban and Elena Hristova

An empty ant track, scuffed by delicate feet.
The violent wind has passed. The hole gapes.
Corn will not sprout under lowering clouds.
The woodpecker's nailed to the bark of a tree.
No one can say what happened to the sky.

I fall to a dark place where words echo.
In the dunes in this well, sand sifts
through the clock of my cupped hands.
Is there any sense in measuring time?

When exposed by rains in an unknown future,
I'll be considered a significant find
as they measure my bones, skull span, and ribs.
No one will know my thoughts about myself.

Refractions

talking of the danger
as if it were not ourselves
as if we were testing anything else
                        — Adrienne Rich

Tell all the Truth but tell it slant—
Success in Circuit lies
                        — Emily Dickinson

S. Ben-Tov

The Summer of the Wild Artichokes

1.

That summer I found
a stain with two red lobes,
a heart's sediment in my underpants.
I carried them to my mother
and we kissed
in the heat of August
in Jerusalem, a kiss
like cool water
tainted with iron.

While the day's strikes over Suez
droned on the radio,
my mother smashed ice with a cleaver
and mashed apricots,
yellow as egg yolks, flecked with red;
the ice cream melting as I served the women
who pressed glasses of iced mint tea
to their brows, and called me "bat mitzvah."

That summer the wild artichokes
muscled their way
through scrub and brambles.
They stood four feet high,
bronze arms, gold-dusted,
their crown of thistle
began to unlock,
the gold fur patch
in the center, spread,
not like sunflowers' platters of seed,
but like suns.

We played paratroopers
in the Valley of the Cross, tumbled
out of olive trees casting
their immature green bullets down.
We scrambled through thistles,

fell into thornbushes,
hung by our knees, imagining
the long roll of sky
around us, and the earth below
winking in the pure light,
a gemmed map
before the scramble into crossfire.

2.

The school nurse comes for all the girls.
We follow her into the clinic.
She draws the shades,
looks outside the door, and locks it.
She tells us there is nothing to be ashamed of.
"Your ovaries are about the size and shape
  of little plums,
    but your womb is like a pear upside-down."

The girls stuff braids into their mouths;
purple shadows quiver in their brown cheeks,
glee darts like fieldmice. Plums! Pears!
One whispers, "Compote,"
they clutch their dark, delicate knees
with white fingertips.
The nurse shrugs.
Soon, she thinks,
you'll be doing the explaining.
"Has any of you begun her bleeding?"

One raises her hand:
a tree has hushed them
in the shade of giant boughs.

During afternoon classes, helicopters
pass overhead, carrying
the wounded back from Sinai.
The sound whips
at the vortex of the sky
like an eggbeater.
As if in heavy fluid
our heads turn to the windows.
The history teacher draws the shades.

S. Ben-Tov

3.

Years later, in America,
I walk into a high school bathroom
which is silent and packed with girls
whose doughy faces are barred
with mascara, who suck
at cigarettes like convicts.
And there it is:
the drag of heavy fluid
toward a vortex where clattering panic
apes the heartbeat.
Someone said someone said a girl died
of lye poured in her womb
by an illegal abortionist.
Her memory seeps into the walls'
gradations of paint,
seeps into the painted faces
grading them with fear.

4.

A bomb blows in the supermarket.
Cases of tomato paste
blast into the street
with splintered sheetglass.
Among the swathes of red gum,
only one woman is hurt.
She lost her husband in '56,
her son in '67; now
she has lost her legs.
Everyone calls her *brave*.

We memorize the names
of things with bombs in them:
purses, buttons, candy, stuffed animals.
Names don't matter —
love, victory, State of Israel —
all wrap bombs. Between
the bomb and the wrapping,
the only thing left
unsuspect, is to act.

5.

In the gorge where we began
our hike: two red cliffs
split by a cataract
laddered with rainbows.
The booming water
filled a deep pool;
I stripped off my khaki
with the others, lying
open-eyed to the blue sky.
The water pounding down its shaft of foam
loaded my heart;
minnows nibbled the hairs
on my legs; when I moved
they drifted like fronds.
The net of being
kisses like sun on water;
then souls can breathe
through pores of rock
or minutes in the skin
of time, easily;
it is easy
to hallucinate words
in that kiss:
singing peels off waterfalls,
the heart's double chant
recalls what is to be.

6.

As we turn this corner
in the mercurial dust of evening
in Jerusalem, or elsewhere,
and you have somewhere to go
from the pitched noon
of your childhood,
and I also have new problems
in old countries,
still,
a word before we go
to light our lamps.

S. Ben-Tov

When they say
"Girls can't be paratroopers",
then you will know
it's too late, because
you walked out
and the street tilted under you;
studied the book
and fell through the lines;
in a word,
you jumped,

jerked the string, got tendons
for floating, and your parachute
englobes slowly like a winged cerebrum.
Whatever fell with you —
scraps of meat,
congealing tears — bat aside.
Now is the time to see
the whole pattern:
sand split with silver deltas,
forests and rivers branching
like neurons, the long scars of roads.
In that pure light
brushed by pinions
you angle toward the curve
crossburned and smoking, small
as a children's ditch,
small as human fury,
and you descend;

when the pure mind falls into battle
knowing what she knows,
the sun's thistles meet her, bronze and gold
with sisters' faces,
as her feet
join their shadows
for the long rush under fire.

William Matthews

Black Box

It's not that the cockpit *fills* with amiable chatter —
for the cockpit, like a snowy village in a paperweight,
is a model of the huge world outside it, and what
but indigenous silence could fill or empty that? —
but that there are wisps of silence in its lofted air:

the sputter and rasp of radio blab, some banter
(this is office life at 39,000 feet), some public
announcements. It's all on actuarial tape, tape
with its slow urinary hiss like the air-filtering
system in a fall-out shelter, as if history

could be survived by its raw materials.
The most frequent last word on the black
box tape is "Mother." Will this change if we get
more female pilots? Who knows? But here's
the best exchange: "We're going down." "I know."

David Ignatow

Sleepy

Now where can I move to get peace,
I already live in the Bronx
near the Yonkers line? I suppose
I could turn off the TV showing
how the bombs fall and explode;
my bed shakes at each impact,
but then there is that funny commercial
following, a fat man astride a balloon
to test its strength, and up it takes him
too late to slip off without falling far,
his eyes wide as balloons, his mouth open
and round, forming his fear, his paunch
pressing up against the sphere, embraced
by his pudgy arms, legs dangling. I hear
a squeaky, comical Help, reminding me
of what I can't say exactly — the stupidity
of the fat man who knows enough to gorge himself? —
the point being that rubber is stronger than ever.

It drifts out of his hands in the force
of the upper currents, and he goes trailing
head over heels in one direction, the balloon
in another; his stomach becomes the whole of him
spinning in the wind as he drifts off
and vanishes into space —
the second commercial message being
that whoever tries to make his weight felt
is going to get a reaction.

Sydney Lea

After Labor Day

Your son is seven years dead.
"But it seems," I said, seeing your face
buckle in mid-conversation
as over the fields came winging the trebles
of children at holiday play —
I said, "But it seems like yesterday."

"No," you said,
"Like today."

In the first of the black fall drizzles,
in a morning when world's-end seems to hover
too near, the early fallen
leaves slick on the highway as blood,
the yellow ball had spun to a halt
on the white line:
your small child scurried there like an ignorant vole...

It is the time of year
when hawks rush down the pass where you live,
but the heat last weekend held them
northward. So grounded, we talked like voluble schoolkids
inside, instead.   —Or I did.
You lost in thought, dark brows arched
like the wings of birds at travel,
or soaring to hide, or seek.

At home, I recall your eagle visage, how now
and then it falls
just so. In the change, in the first cold autumn rain,
I play at identification.
I imagine how Redtail, Cooper's,
Roughleg, Little Blue Darter,
and the odd outsider —Swainson's, say—
now pass you by,
as at home in my study I watch
two scruffy starlings on a wire outside

fronting what they seem to have
no choice but to front
till one peels off, is sucked it seems into woods, and through
the glass I yet can hear him.
His croaks come this way, as if the other
were the one who had vanished, not he.

Just so lost children imagine
their parents are lost, not they.
"Where did you go?" they chirp, as if we hadn't been
shrieking, searching.
Or as if our terror had been a game.

It's the season of the mushroom all of a sudden.

Closed though my window is,
over the vapors and trees I also hear
the doubled scream of a kestrel.

You heard, these seven years have heard, the swish
of tandem tires through puddles,
the last gasps
of airbrakes, screams.
And loud as unthinkable detonation
—or so at least in dreams it seems—
the impact:

every outside sound raced clear to you.
But walls and panes cut short your shouts
from inside the house,
as if *you* were the small boy
to whom the remote roar
of the world was suddenly apparent,
yet whose voice was as in dreams
unheard or worse: irrelevant.

In the lulls, by way of compensation,
I talked the holiday away.
Talked and talked and
talked and talked
and catalogued the game:

I called attention
to early Goldeneyes out on the marsh;
to the way in later light
—like cheap raincoats— the feather's colors
on the backs of seaducks would change and change;
and, higher, to the cloud that would mean this greater
    change,
swooping against the yellow ball of the sun.

As if through a shield of thin glass,
there was the further drone of the bomber whereby,
you said, "One day the world will be lost,"

and the bitter joke, I understood,
be on those of us who all these seasons
have played at discourse.
"Where did you go?"
So the world will ask.

Howard Moss

Einstein's Bathrobe

I wove myself of many delicious strands
Of violet islands and sugar balls of thread
So faintly green a small white check between
Balanced the field's wide lawn, a plaid
Gathering in loose folds shaped around him
Those Princeton mornings, slowly stage-lit, when
The dawn took the horizon by surprise
And from the marsh long, crayoned birds
Rose up, ravens, maybe crows, or raw-voiced,
Spiteful grackles with their clothespin legs,
Black-winged gossips rising out of mud
And clattering into sleep. They woke my master
While, in the dark, I waited, knowing
Sooner or later he'd reach for me
And, half asleep, wriggle into my arms.
Then it seemed a moonish, oblique light
Would gradually illuminate the room,
The world turn on its axis at a different slant,
The furniture a shipwreck, the floor askew,
And, in old slippers, he'd bumble down the stairs.
Genius is human and wants its coffee hot—
I remember mornings when he'd sit
For hours at breakfast, dawdling over notes,
Juice and toast at hand, the world awake
To spring, the smell of honeysuckle
Filling the kitchen. A silent man,
Silence became him most. How gently
He softened   the edges of a guessed-at impact
So no one would keel over from the blow—
A blow like soft snow falling on a lamb.
He'd fly down from the heights to tie his shoes
And cross the seas to get a glass of milk,
Bismarck with a harp, who'd doff his hat
(As if he ever wore one!) and softly land
On nimble feet so not to startle. He walked
In grandeur much too visible to be seen—
And how many versions crawled out into the Press!

A small pre-Raphaelite with too much hair;
A Frankenstein of test tubes; a "refugee"—
A shaman full of secrets, who could touch
Physics with a wand and body forth
The universe's baby wrapped in stars.
From signs Phoenicians scratched into the sand
With sticks he drew the contraries of space:
Whirlwind Nothing and Volume in its rage
Of matter racing to undermine itself,
And when the planets sang, why, he sang back
The lieder black holes secretly adore.

At tea at Mercer Street every afternoon
His manners went beyond civility,
Kindness not having anything to learn;
I was completely charmed. And fooled.
What a false view of the universe *I* had!
The horsehair sofa, the sagging chairs,
A fire roaring behind the firescreen—
Imagine thinking Princeton was the world!
Yet I wore prescience like a second skin:
When Greenwich and Palomar saw eye to eye,
Time and space having found their rabbi,
I felt the dawn's black augurs gather force,
As if I knew in the New Jersey night
The downcast sky that was to clamp on Europe,
That Asia had its future in my pocket.

Leonard Nathan

One Vote

What we cannot imagine but know somehow to be true — like death or the possibility of nuclear war — affects us in ways that are hard to define because the effects are often indirect, as when otherwise harmless objects terrorize us in dreams and leave behind echoes of the same terror when we awaken. Indirection seems to be the only unhysterical way we can deal with the terrible but true. That is why perhaps the best modern poetry about death and cataclysm is indirect. The poem about nuclear destruction I am most moved by is William Stafford's "At the Bomb Testing Site."

> At noon in the desert a panting lizard
> waited for history, its elbows tense,
> watching the curve of a particular road
> as if something might happen.
>
> It was looking at something farther off
> than people could see, an important scene
> acted in stone for little selves
> at the flute end of consequences.
>
> There was just a continent without much on it
> under a sky that never cared less.
> Ready for a change, the elbows waited.
> The hands gripped hard on the desert.
>   (*West of Your City*, Talisman Press, 1960)

The poem never alludes directly to its subject except in the title. The awful potential is seen through the anticipatory behavior of the lizard, and described with understated detachment. Direct treatment of such subjects tends to be shrilly trite, hysterically accusing, and sometimes merely self-pitying, as though, in search of terms congruent with the magnitude of the unspeakable, writers pass beyond the limits of what they can control by art and intelligence. I think it was the philosopher Adorno who, after World War II, proclaimed: "No poems about concentration camps!" Although I'm put off by his peremptory tone and his implication that there are subjects too serious for the self-indulgence of poets, I think I understand what prompted such an utterance. In a time when so much poetry contains, as a sort of authenticating credential, the personality of the poet, the treatment of really tremendous topics deserves something better than pathetic personal stance, more or less grandiose. In this century, American poets don't seem to have the powers for voicing serious public outrage, public grief or joy — the price we pay, I suppose, for our poetic tradition having rooted itself in subjectivity as the only authentic ground for poetry. One of the results of this aesthetic decision — which is part of the inheritance of the Romantic movement — is that whenever poets begin to write about some public issue, it is difficult for them not to conclude by assimilating it to their personal lives. This is as true of Carolyn Forché as it was for Wordsworth, though Wordsworth still had available to him poetic conventions that allowed him to generalize subjectivity into something like a public self. Most poets have long ago forsaken such conventions as being the mark of rhetorical bluster and eloquent mendacity. With the more modest instruments of a small lyric voice, contemporary poets do what they can, but what they cannot do very well, it seems, is move into the public domain without feeling self-conscious or clumsily defiant. And this, I think, is why a poem like Stafford's seems memorable. It is able to shift its subjectivity to another creature — a creature noted for its cold blood — and offer instinctual anticipation as a kind of measure for the unspeakable.

I am not against directness and my wincing at what seems to be the general badness of poems that directly address horror may only be the reflex of aesthetic bias. But I am against bad rhetoric in a good cause, that is, rhetoric which leaves untouched or alienates the very audience it meant to move to its view. The question to be asked here is: what can contemporary poetry do and to whom can it do it? It can, I think, make some see who don't and remind some who can, to look again. But this seeing takes considerable precision; otherwise, the poet is nothing more or less than a propagandist (and, I submit, usually an inferior one to those trained in the field). A trouble here is that not many people read poetry. I have received scratched-up *ad hoc* broadsides containing fifteen or twenty anti-nuclear poems, usually shoddy work, sometimes by good poets. I read them. Other poets read them. We all agree — nuclear war is terrible. Something must be done. But the same effect can be, and often is, achieved in a newspaper editorial, which reaches a wider audience, some of whom do not agree or hardly think about agreement or disagreement. Between the value of the two kinds of protests, I'll pick the editorial every time. The anti-nuclear poems seem, next to a halfway decent newspaper article, hoarse sighs in the wilderness. It is as if American poets, in order to be believed, have to scream (lucky Russian poets; they can be hauled in for a subversive whisper). But American poets are *not* believed because they are not read — at least by the audience that their political poems aim to persuade. Since pupils, disciples, fellow poets are already persuaded, what then is the point, except to clear a heavy conscience or relieve a frustrated passion to DO something?

For all the dozens of anti-nuclear poems I have read and for-gotten, Stafford's sticks in my mind (along with Karl Shapiro's wonderful "The Progress of Faust") not just as a clever handling of a difficult topic, but as some measure for the magnitude of the danger, a magnitude I can handle at least with some sense that I can act on it, in however limited a way, and can act, so far as it is in my power to, rationally. Direct poems on the topic usually leave me with one of two feelings, if they don't put me off altogether: either I feel helpless before what they prophecy or I feel like rushing out and doing *something* fast; since there is nothing useful like that to do, this latter feeling itself leads to a sense of futility and finally indifference. I begin to think of something else, something less paralyzing, and leave it to dreams to remind me of the unspeakable.

I do not rule out that ideal: a great public poem on this issue, speaking in powerful, widely-understandable ways about nuclear war, a poem that, like Dostoyevski's *House of the Dead*, might significantly revolutionize behavior. But I doubt it. What I do not doubt is that effective poems can be written on the un-speakable. They may seem modest, perhaps innocuous, because they work through indirection, not startling us to mindless action like a siren charging through our sleep, but subtly shifting the way we see the reality, keeping our imagination alive to possi-bilities. And perhaps — though this may be wishful thinking — spreading through a wider consciousness than that represented by the tiny audience for poetry.

When I show those who are not poetry readers the Stafford poem, show it and try to explain how it works, they usually become thoughtful. I want them to be thoughtful, not to knock me down and run for the nearest exit. I think that's the best we can hope for — that a lot of people become thoughtful. Let them be scared too (and perhaps direct poems can have some effect here), but let them be thinking hard. That seems to me the first step toward serious argument and useful action. And I don't know what else or what better we can hope for out of all this. And after all, it may actually come down to one vote.

How did the stones vote
this time?

They voted for hardness
and few words

as the trees voted
for slow growth
upward and a shedding
of dead dependents.

And the men?

They voted against
themselves again
and for fire
which they thought they
could control,
fire
which voted for blackened stumps
and no more elections.

"The Election," by Leonard Nathan, from *Dear Blood*, University of Pittsburgh Press, 1980.

Carolyn Ross

New Houses

In 1957, when I was six, my family moved into a modern split-level ranch house with open beams and kitchen counters the color of Campbell's Tomato Soup, and an expanse of glass overlooking Dishwater Run. When I entered first grade the house was at the edge of a cow pasture and a corn field, and by the time I went downtown to junior high we were enveloped by a bona fide housing development.

Those were boom years. World War II — even Korea — seemed as far away then as they do now, and the smells of freshly milled wood and new paint were everywhere. Everything was new: there was the "new store" and the "new school," always another "new road," and in the "new houses" a growing band of neighborhood children played. In the skeletal pattern of rooms, we acted out our ideas of domesticity: we cooked and we cleaned, we lay on beds of insulation and two-by-fours. On rainy days we gathered on the dirt floors of crawl spaces, and in the fall we raked leaves into piles and leapt from second storeys. During school hours and until five we allowed the workmen to make their changes, but for weekends and evenings the new houses were ours.

When a house grew beyond us, with windows and doors that closed and locked, we lifted the floorboards and withdrew our caches of candy and small change, comics and jelly jars, and we moved on to the next new house, the next arrangement of rooms. I dreamed of houses then, as I do now — new houses, old houses, houses I recognized, houses I had never seen before, houses in which I discovered secret passageways and secret rooms in which I found monsters and angels.

One October day in 1962 we were sitting on the floor of what would soon be a stranger's living room when my mother appeared, from the waist up, in the empty rectangular space of a front doorway. No parent had ever intruded at any of our houses. Their voices had always been enough to draw us home across the broken ground and new sod of our lots. I was surprised and angry that she even knew of this secret place; but her face was stricken, and her voice so quiet it occurred to me that someone had died. She said, "I want you home now. The rest of you, go home too." There was no question of resistance.

At home we found my father filling gallon milk bottles with tap water and putting cans of hash and mixed vegetables and dog food into grocery bags. We all carried things down to the basement where my mother set up sleeping bags for my brother and me among paint cans and garden tools. And there we spent the night, listening to the radio. That was the Cuban Missile Crisis, when we were led to believe that we could survive a nuclear war with our backs to a basement wall.

When I began junior high school in 1963, housing starts were down in our neighborhood, not because of an inhospitable economy, but because there was little room left for more new houses. The cows who had for years huddled under a lone elm tree in their shrinking pasture were long gone, and the corn fields had retreated to the other side of the valley.

Although there were younger kids who sometimes played with us, we were the oldest, the originals: Bobby, Linda, her brother Richie, and I. At parties in garages and rec rooms we started dancing close, to Frankie Valli and the Four Seasons, to the Everley Brothers. We considered kisses. Our play sessions at the new houses were exclusive and full of sexual tension. There were games of hide-and-seek and chase, the boys always the seekers and chasers, and at moments when pursuit became embrace, no one knew how to end the game. Across stacks of lumber we wrestled to disguise our caresses.

On November 22, 1963, John F. Kennedy was assassinated by Lee Harvey Oswald. Two days later, in the Thanksgiving chill of an unfinished house, the four of us took off our clothes and touched one another. I was unfamiliar even with the body of another girl and was astonished by the sight of small breasts where I had only buds. The boys' penises were shriveled, old-looking, and we brushed them quickly with our fingertips. We did not want them to know that inside the folds of skin we had vaginas. We dressed again in cold and silence.

That day I found blood on my underpants. I remember lying across my parents' bed watching my mother absently dress as she followed on television the transfer of Lee Harvey Oswald to the Dallas County Jail. She put on her bra, her slip, her close-fitting dress that held the shape of her bosom even as it hung on its hanger. I felt ashamed — of my maturity, my immaturity. I remember waiting and not wanting to tell her how I'd grown. I remember deciding not to, never to, and, turning, I saw Jack Ruby emerge from a crowd of reporters and shoot Lee Harvey Oswald dead.

Carolyn Ross

The distinction between life and television drama was not altogether clear to me, and it took some time for the realities of having seen a real murder committed on television, and of having changed forever, to sink in.

I recently visited my old neighborhood for the first time since I'd left at the age of fourteen. The development had leapt the natural boundaries of forest and creek like a fire jumping a fireline. Some of the original houses, like ours, looked a bit ragged, comically "modern" archetypes. At the new peripheries of the development were a few abandoned housing starts. Windows had been broken by objects thrown through them, and chain-link fences had been erected with padlocked gates to keep out vandals. The developer had faltered in bankruptcy.

As I passed Bobby's old house I saw his mother standing on the front steps applying a new coat of paint to the front door, so I stopped to say hello. She told me that Robert had just published his first novel, that Linda had become an obstetrician, but that Richie had drowned several years earlier off a Florida beach.

That night I dreamed that Richie and I were making love on a plywood floor under a windy star-filled November sky, in a room defined only by the skeletal walls of a new house, while its struts and beams shook and a padlock clanked at the gate.

Madeline DeFrees

The Leper Graves at Spinalonga

The holy ones, lives written after on the skull
would be off-limits here
where lepers with more money sleep in private
graves. Their skeletons fare worse
than those who lie together: lids pried loose
by marauders from the artificial
caves, wood left to warp in sun. They hawk
the skulls like trophies in the town
across the water until Greek fathers lay down laws
to fence them out.

          The life already written on
my skull, still thatched with hair, at last
uncovered to the sun,
engraves the body deeper every year, the air
ecstatic with the prize
not won. Slowly from this peninsula, the eye
clones a circle to its frame. The algebraic
bones assemble in the well,
the femoral declares itself, and memory
retrieves its thoughtful home.

          I'd like to play
the prophet in the valley of this death,
call each spine and clavicle
by name: announce, *In spite of all, these bones
will live again, be covered with
new skin, the slain
come back an army, and from the four winds,
breath*. All make-believe I know.
Dry as we are, as good as dead, can anything begin
the slow articulation led by light?

          The toe
I broke last summer looks shorter knit
together where I climbed the stone in sandals,

a maimed evangelist in Spinalonga
on the run. Back home our leaders lie together,
their plots more private than the leper graves
and not in Arlington. The long disease
continues, fences collapse and walls, no matter
how we guard them. We peddle artifacts
staring from the crater. We are happy
vandals writing history on skulls.

Peter Makuck

Stephen Judy's Execution, That Night

His face fills the screen,
famous a little longer with its smile
and canine teeth, big like mine.

He looks into and through the camera
at all the late-night drinkers and snackers,
without remorse, determined to die.

Pitilessly, he smiles
and they cut to a room, all bars and shadows
where death has built a late-night throne,
a future for itself.

Judy grins.
My armchair gives a jolt.

*

I leave the house
like a country I no longer love.

The moon advertises a better life.
One by one, streets and sleeping windows fall away,
arguments for and against.

I come to a fence, a wide tobacco field.
There is one light
in a tenant shack, far on the other side.
A man, perhaps, with a cigarette
plotting a future, his lungs feeding on dreams
of profit and loss.

*

The quarter moon
smiles sharply at a life with others.

There's a point in Defoe's island book
where Crusoe contemplates the reef and the new wreck
and realizes that one man's safety
is another's destruction.

Or an animal's perhaps.
The fox I shotgunned in the yard once: rabies,
a red plot against the snow, something or other.
That night I wasn't safe. My hands
lay like animals barely tamed at my sides.

*

His foster mother begged
he be kept alive and studied . . .

The smallest cells, lethal genes, the secret
circuitry of his behavior
all beg to be understood.

Peter Makuck

The night's electric blue.
                    Past Saturn
a probe moves us to the fringes of what we know.

I stand here watching the light in that shack.
Everything is reduced to that one light,
warm, yellow, alive, and oddly poignant
across the field. Suddenly
there's darkness where it was.

*

Some people can't sleep.
There's a woman in curlers
smoking and reading *People*.
She takes a deep drag at the sight of Cher,
that lovely house and California pool . . .

Is it a noise that makes her cock her head and stand?
The window holds a moon with a pitiless hooked up smile.
She drops the shade.

That creaking noise?
An orange face on the talkshow
thinks it's all a scream
and cracks up soundlessly.

William Carpenter

Landscape with Figures

A boy stands in a field in Massachusetts, beside
his father, who is at an easel, painting what they
see: the summer house, the harbor with its boats,

the dunes reaching beyond Truro to Provincetown.
Night after night, he's had the same dream, someone
with a mask walking behind him in an empty bedroom,

and when he turns around, it's his own face, only
different, in the same way the painting differs
from the afternoon. His father changes things,

moves them around, so that the neighbors' cottage
has become a boulder, so that a lighthouse grows
out of the bare sand. The boy is angry with

the picture, because it is not real. He turns away
to watch his mother, her arms full of white shirts,
pinning them to the clothesline so the wind fills

them like a flock of heavy teachers trying to fly.
His father paints her, paints the row of shirts,
wipes his brush, walks over as if to help her, but

they start fighting again, and the boy sees shirts
blowing across the poison ivy, along the beach.
One of the shirts blows in the water as if someone

had drowned and was drifting in with the high tide.
When his father hits her, she cries out once with
the same cry that the herring gulls use during a

storm, then she grows smaller; she lies down like
an empty shirt in the mown field. His father walks
away, stands on the beach, raises both arms as if

he could erase the sunset, could submerge the last
children on the diving float, who are even now
pushing each other in and laughing because they

can't see what is happening: the woman rising to
her feet, wiping her blue skirt as she walks out
to join her husband; the boy making an orange stripe

on the unfinished landscape, with the largest brush,
like a meteor only in broad daylight, like a story
of the sun falling and falling till it hits the sea.

Another of my poems, "Fire," has a more overt level of anti-confrontation senti-
ment; but upon thinking about "Landscape with Figures" again, I realize why
you would choose it. It's pretty difficult for most poets to participate in the nuclear
protest with their work—it's just not a time for propaganda in poetry—but I
do think that most good writing at this time must show at some level the urgen-
cy of this historic context. This particular poem, like several others I've been
working on recently, and like some I've seen by other poets, has a strain of violence
which does not come from my life directly but which must reflect the deeper
background...When they asked Carl Jung if he thought we could survive the
nuclear age, he gave the rather cryptic response, "only if man can contain the
Opposites within his own mind." I think poetry, like all of the arts, is a way
of making this containment and of giving the forms of violence an operational
field. In my case, the poem is of the nuclear family and its barely-controlled
power—which I think has a more than analogical relationship to the forces within
the atom.

Amy Clampitt

A New Life

Autonomy these days — surprise! — is moving up
in the corporate structure. She's thrown over
the old laid-back lifestyle, repudiated its
green-haired prophets, and gotten married

(pre-Raphaelite red velvet, a sheaf of roses,
hair falling in two long blond tresses). She's
now at home on a rural route, its row of mailboxes
a mile and a half from the Freeway. Not-quite-

two-year-old Autonomy Junior spends long days
with the sitter, can count up to five, and sees
the world moving past so fast, he delivers daily
not slow words but quick, predicated word-clusters.

Up before dawn three days out of five, at the
bathroom mirror Autonomy swiftly, with brush and
hairdryer, concocts a frame for her face of that
temporal gold, like the gilding of the aspens

in the Rockies, like every prototypical true
blonde who began as some other color; puts on
her boardroom clothes — flounced denim with
boots and weskit, or spiked sandals and pallid

executive knit — to drive off into the just-
stirred mother-of-pearl of the day, the velour
of hoarfrost's transient platinum on the blacktop
no more lush than the pristine pale upholstery

of the brand-new Brougham — into the ductile realm
of the Freeway, that reentry into the mystery of
being betweenwheres, alone in the effortless
anteroom of the Machine, of the Many. The Company

these days is paying her way to an earlybird
course in Econ at the University. At eight-
thirty, while her wedded bedfellow, in the other
car, the red Toyota, drops off their offspring

with the sitter, her class over, she's taking
the Freeway again to headquarters. These days
she's in Quality Circles, a kind of hovering
equipoise between Management and not-Management,

precarious as the lake-twinned tremor of aspens,
as the lingering of the ash-blond arcade of foliage
completing itself as it leans to join its mirror-
image. Whatever fabrication, whatever made thing

she is thus vertiginously linked to, there's no
disconnecting the image of Autonomy contained but
still moving — toward what is unclear — up through
the heady apertures of the Gross National Product,

from that thing, the ambiguous offspring of the Company —
through whose dense mansions, burbling the unheard melodies
of the new, her pal and bedfellow is moving up too.
Evenings, while he heads for *his* course at the Univers-

ity, she collects the not-yet-two-year-old from the
sitter, kicks off her stiltwalker's footgear, peels
away the layers of the persona of Quality Circles,
and slides into irontight jeans, the time-honored

armor of mellowing out; picks up yesterday's litter from
around the playpen, puts together a quick concoction
via the microwave oven, and resumes — her charge,
all the while, voluble at her hip or underfoot —

the improbable game of move and countermove between
mother-and-child. Whether, back at headquarters,
back there in the winking imaginary map that leaps
from the minds of the computer programmers, there's

a mother-lode of still smarter bombs, the germ
of an even cleverer provocation to instability

within the neutron or of God knows what other, yet
inviolate speck at the core of the cosmos, who knows? —

or whether playing at mothering, the mirage of a
rise into ethereal realms of the managerial — of
hoarfrost at dawn along the edge of the Freeway,
the hurtled ease of finding oneself betweenwheres,

alone in the evolving anteroom of the Machine, of
that artifice of the pursuit of happiness — will be,
as the green-haired prophets of punk would have it,
a total, or only a partial
                    apocalyptic freakout.

John Haines

Death is a Meadowlark

Memorials and Consolations From a Work In Progress

Long before I went to live in the woods my awareness of death
seemed to have a depth beyond any exact recall. It existed as
a memory composed of discontinuous images: a snake crushed
on the summer roadway, reeking in the sun — how dull and
flattened it was compared to the live snake, supple and glisten-
ing, I had seen in the grass a week before. A drowned and
bloated frog I had pulled from the bottom of a backyard

117

pool and held in my hand: a wonder — why did it not breathe? A bird in whose decaying nostrils small white worms were coiling. These were the naked things of an uninstructed child-hood in which there was little instinctive fear.

And had I not seen as a child the crushed body of a woman sprawled on the city curbing? She had jumped from a window ledge many stories above, and lay concealed by the brown heap of her clothing. Nothing else was visible from where I stood, clutched by my mother on a crowded downtown street. There had been the sound of a scream, a sudden rush of air, a glimpse of a spread shape flying down, and the thudding shock of her landing. I was hurried away, and I saw no more.

And there had been also my own near death by drowning late in the first decade of my life. Death had taken the form of a watery green darkness into which I was sinking, slowed and numbed by the depth and cold, while above me the strange, lost sight of sunlight faded from the surface.

It was not then, but a later time, when I was about thirteen. We lived on the edge of uninhabited countryside at the end of a street in suburban California. From our backyard a pathway led uphill into open fields.

One Sunday morning in spring, after the family had returned from church and we had eaten a late breakfast, I went for a long walk alone over the fields. I do not remember what was on my mind then, confused by the unsorted emotions of youth or, as it may have been, delighting in the open sky and the sun on the warm grasses.

The pathway soon merged with a narrow country road. The bare soil in the wheeltracks was damp from the winter rains, and there was an occasional shallow pool of water in a deeper rut. As I came over the crest of the hill I saw something lying at the side of the road just ahead of me. When I came up to it, I saw that it was a rabbit, and that it was dead. Its brown and white fur was torn and its belly ripped open.

I came closer and stopped before it. Just for a moment I stood there looking down at the torn, but still intact animal. The blue bulge of its gut lay half-spilled from the body and shone brightly, glazed with blood, in the morning sunlight. A few flies already buzzed around it.

A nameless panic gripped me. I heard the buzzing of the flies and other insects, and somewhere close but out of sight a meadowlark was singing. There was nothing else around, no other sign of man, of animal or bird of prey. Beyond the hill crest not even a housetop showed above the yellow grasses. I was alone under the sun in an open field with death, unmistakeable, physical death.

It was not just that still form lying at the edge of the road, nor the blood that was dried upon its fur; I had seen things like it before. It was something new — an awakening that fastened on the incredible shining blueness of the inside turned outside, the innermost part ripped from its place and spilled into the light where it did not belong. Gazing, fixed before it in the morning sunlight, I felt perhaps for the first time, an absolute aloneness. And I who at that age loved solitude, knew that this was death, the loneliest solitude of all.

In terror I began to walk, away from that scene, over the grassy slope of the hill, but looking behind me all the while as if I expected that quiet, mutilated form to rise from the damp ground and follow me. Perhaps I feared that somewhere in that silent, sunny countryside, in the grass, even in the voice of the meadowlark, death itself was waiting.

I do not know what sermon I had half-listened to that morning in church; something that had deepened my mood and prompted my walk — something about mortality, was it, of death and the hereafter, of reward and damnation? I don't remember. Yet somehow I felt deeply that I was guilty, but of what I did not know.

I walked a long way that morning, troubled and confused. I returned over the same path on my way home. As fearful as I had been, both repelled and attracted, I had to see that form of death again. I had to know.

But when I came again to that place in the road, on the rounded hilltop, there was nothing there. I looked around, thinking I had mistaken the location, and that the dead rabbit was somewhere close by. Its absence now was even more alarming. Had I really seen it? But yes, for here in the brown soil at the edge of the grass was a small, darkened spot that appeared to be blood, and near it a little patch of rabbit fur.

I struggled with explanations. Something — hawk or fox — disturbed originally by my coming, had run off and left its victim in the road. And when I had gone, it returned to claim its food.

Still the feeling of dread remained as I walked on toward home. I think now that I told no one of what I had seen, but kept it as a secret, something shared between me, the grass, and the unseen meadowlark. The impression of that morning stayed with me for a long time, and for a while I avoided that part of the road on my walks. When later I crossed the hill at that spot, alone or with friends, I half-expected to see the rabbit again, to have it rise before me from the grass without warning, and with that large, incredibly distended bulge of its stomach, veined with fat, gleaming so brightly blue and green in the sun. But a ghost-image was all I had; a latent emotion charged with mistrust, and a lingering fear.

Transitory in the field, under the sun, slowly disintegrating under blows of the summer rain, an image of the world's stupendous accident. An instant of inexplicable calm, as on the bright, cold winter day I found a redpoll frozen on a snowbank at the entrance to the homestead road. There was nothing to tell me how the bird came to die there. It may have been stunned by the wind gust from a passing car, or it may have fallen asleep while feeding on the blown seeds of the few weed stalks that showed above the snow, and momentarily warming itself in the cold sun. There was not a mark on its body, not a feather disturbed. Under the downy fluff the tiny feet were stiffened; the eyes were half-closed and crystallized, at either side of the nostrils lay a delicate whisker of frost. The rusty crown of its head was bright with color, and the flushed breast seemed almost warm to my touch. But it was absolutely still, the breast and the heart within it joined in a lump of ice. I held the bird for a moment before putting it to rest again in the snow. It seemed to weigh nothing at all.

In that tiny, quenched image of vitality, a bird like a leaf dropped by the wind in passing, I felt something of our common, friable substance — a shared vulnerability grasped once with insight and passion, and then too easily forgotten. Necessarily forgotten, perhaps, for to keep such a thing constantly before one might be intolerable; the identification would wound too deeply.

I see again the worn, chalk-white skull of a caribou left behind on the fall tundra many years ago. One half of an antler poked up from the deep moss in which the skull was lying; the moss and the accumulation of old leaves and plant debris had nearly buried the rest of it from view.

When I tilted the skull slightly, I saw that a thin, green mold clung to the bone below the soil line. There had been no trace there for a long time of meat, of marrow or gristle. All else was bleached, chalky and crumbling: the upper jaw with a few loose molars, the long thin nostril bone, the eye-sockets, and the mouldering hollows behind the ears. The remaining antler revealed the worn tooth-marks of rodents who in past years, when the skull was still fresh, had gnawed it for the calcium in the bone.

The small lichens and the mosses that had taken root upon the skull were breaking down whatever was left of its structure. It seemed to me as I walked away and turned to view it from a little distance, that the skull was like a small vessel, abandoned by captain and crew; rudderless and demasted, it was sinking into the moss and frozen sod. The wet, green sea-life of the tundra washed over the pale wreck in tiny waves year after year, and sooner or later sun, rain and frost would claim it completely. Farewell.

On a snowy day early in October I was sitting at breakfast alone in the house at Richardson, gloomy with the knowledge that the moose season had closed and I had yet to get my meat for the winter. I had hunted for better than two weeks, all through the cool, dry days of late September, and had seen nothing but tracks. Winter was coming, there was snow on the ground, nearly eight inches of it already, and I knew that in order to find a moose now I would have to go far into the hills for it, and by the time I got it, late in the rut, the meat was sure to be lean and tough.

As I was cleaning up the breakfast pans and dishes, I thought I heard a sound outside, rather like a low grunt, and one of the dogs chained in the yard gave a sharp "woof." I went to the door and looked out. To my astonishment I saw a large bull moose stalking slowly uphill through the snowy garden.

The moose, plainly in view against the white, cleared ground, paused and looked down toward the house and yard. In those few moments of what seemed to be a kind of mutual recognition, it struck me that the moose was not in the best of condition, that perhaps it had been beaten in a fight, or was overtaken by weariness. But no matter — here was my meat, and right in the yard.

I had a rifle at my hand, but at that moment a car went by on the road below the house, driving slowly because of the fresh snowfall. As keenly as I wanted that moose, I feared that it would be seen if I shot it there in plain view and out of season. I waited, and watched the moose climb the open hill and go out of sight over the crest toward the potato patch.

I decided immediately to follow it, to take another way up the hill and head it off, since the moose seemed to be in no hurry. I dressed myself quickly in overshoes, cap, jacket and gloves, and with the rifle in hand I took off up the hill through the falling snow.

I climbed through the woods, following a trail I had cut the year before. I did not dare to stop for rest, but plowed on, hoping that the snowfall and the laden branches would dampen any sound I was making. In a short time I reached the top of a narrow ridge where the trail began to level off. And there I found the tracks of the moose who had just passed before me. He could not be far ahead. Panting, stumbling at times in the fresh snow, I followed those tracks, determined to catch up with that moose or fall in the snow from trying.

Within a quarter of a mile I came to place where the trail straightened and I could see some distance ahead of me. Another twenty yards, and I caught up with the moose, now a large brown bulk blurred by the falling snow, standing in the birches. He was stopped in the trail, his head half-turned, looking back in my direction.

Trembling from the long climb, I raised the rifle, trying for some kind of shooting rest against the nearest tree. As I was doing this, the moose, alerted now, broke into a trot and began to move swiftly ahead. I had no time for a better shot; he would soon be out of sight, and I was too badly winded from the climb to pursue him any further. I aimed for a spot just below the tail stump and fired.

At the sound of the shot the moose jumped, ran forward at a faster pace, and stopped. As I approached him, he turned to one side of the trail and stepped slowly into the woods, as if he would think awhile on what had happened. In the one large, dark eye turned toward me I could see a kind of blunted panic and bewilderment. I was ready to shoot again, not knowing if I really had him, when he staggered, felt for better footing, and fell heavily on his right side with a soft, cushioned *swoosh*, sending a shower of dry snow into the air. Once he tried to raise his head, then let it fall. As I came near I saw his chest heave out a mighty sigh, and one leg stiffen slightly. And then the woods were silent in the falling snow.

The open eye of the moose gazed blank and dull into the tree-stroked whiteness. A few wet flakes fell on the eyelids, melted on the warm nostrils, and sank into the long, unmoving ears.

The great, dark bulk was still. I felt, as I always do at such times, a strange and painful combination of emotions, if what one feels then can be called emotion precisely — a mingling of awe, of regret, of elation and relief. There was a quiet space in which to breathe, to acknowledge that something urgent and needed had been accomplished, all anxiety and uncertainty for the moment done with.

I returned down the snowy trail to the house to get my knife, my axe and saw, and a length of rope. And once more up the trail, I was soon at work on the carcass. First, I cut off the head with its heavy antlers. Then I tied a foreleg to a tree, and pushed and balanced the heavy, inert bulk onto its back. As always, it was strenuous work for a single man. But now death was forgotten. A transformation had taken place, and what had been a vital and breathing creature, capable of perception and of movement, was now only meat and salvage — a hairy mound of bone and muscle.

When I cut through the hide and strained inner tissue of the paunch, a cloud of red steam burst on the snowy air. And soon I could see deep into the steaming red cavity divided from the upper torso by the taut, muscular wall of the diaphragm. Working by feel alone in the hot soupiness of the rib cage, I loosened the windpipe, then pulled the stomach and the intestines clear, tumbling the heavy, stretched bag and ropy folds onto the snow. There was no fat on the veil nor around the kidneys, but I had not expected to find any. The meat would be lean, but it was better than no meat at all.

And now, with the entire inner part open to the light, I found that my single bullet had traveled the length of the body cavity, just under the spine, and had cut the blood vessels around the heart. Death had been swift, and little meat was spoiled.

That afternoon I dragged the quarters downhill through the snow and hung them on the rack behind the house. A week later a strong wind blew from the south, much of the snow melted, and a springlike warmth sailed through the woods. Where the killed moose had lain, the shaded snow thawed, then froze again, forming a kind of sunken circle that was stained pink and yellow, and matted with hair and leaves. It was soon to be covered by a fresh snowfall, and in a far month to come, to melt and be once more a part of the spring earth.

I have taken the pages of my contribution to this gathering from a chapter I have been writing, and which is essentially a meditation on death. It seems to me that it is this that lies at the heart of the question we are asked: death, and one's attitude toward this elemental event. To give an answer to the question asked is to answer a question in myself. As I prepare to enter my sixth decade, I am acutely aware that the time is limited, that before me somewhere lies death, and whether it comes in sleep, in the slow wasting of pain, or in a violent form is not primarily a matter of individual choice.

I would like to think, therefore, that a part of my answer could be that the possibility of annihilation does not affect me at all, since it has in a sense always been there. I would like to say that my perception of life and experience remains the same, that the world of nature has not changed for me, and that the purpose (in part the naming and celebration of a familiar landscape) that has brought me this far remains steady and sustaining.

But I find that this is only partly true. Nuclear threat aside, I am all too aware of changes in the world during my lifetime, changes that make any innocence or optimism regarding the forces at work among us impossible to maintain.

I am old enough to remember the 1930s and the approach of a war in which I took part. It seems to me that my childhood and early youth took place in an interval of truce during which many smaller wars were fought, and people everywhere lived with much inherited misery. The smoke column that was to rise over Hiroshima was a larger version of the clouds that smothered Shanghai, Chungking, and later Warsaw. I hope not to see, not even in photographs or on the screen, the dead and the maimed, the driven homeless of still another major episode.

And yet my sense of things tells me that the relative security of this society cannot hold, and that a debt remains to be paid to this century out of the safety we have so far contrived.

The trend toward general disorder and breakdown, the apparent futility of traditional political gestures, the frantic determination to discover and exploit to the utmost every available material resource; the deliberate promotion of appetite, the corrosive competitiveness that leaks into every corner of life — all seem to serve a ferocious will to excess, violence and extinction of hope, as if what it amounted to was a kind of revenge on life, and in which we are all implicated. A withering in the gaze of so many people: Hysteria camped in the soul's desert, with a dead fire to warm itself.

How do I feel about the prospect that much of the life of this planet will suffer enormous losses because of our interference? How does this affect my writing? Or is it that this threat is only a further consequence of the measures we have been putting into effect for thousands of years—is the "logical conclusion" of these?

I tell myself that earth has seen far greater catastrophes than any we can devise—ages of volcanic fire, of sulfur, of ice, inundation and upheaval — and survived them all. I feel sure that it will again, if that *again* takes the form of human intervention on colossal scale. Whatever humanity may come to, whatever device it may explode, new forms are possible, new life always, and nothing we can do will cancel this.

Seen from sufficient perspective, it is all right if the volcano blows its tops, if villages and cities are buried in ash, mud and debris; though people die and are scattered, the ash and mud settle into place, and sooner or later the land is refreshed, and things flower again. Only wait.

I can be persuaded that Western Civilization will one day cease to exist, whether that end comes in the slow attrition of centuries or as a succession of violent blows, and I am not greatly disturbed by the prospect. Fixed in the immobility of its forms, life becomes a museum of itself; any fresh conception must make its way by whatever means, by infiltration or with dynamite, in a sometimes bitter tonic of revival.

There is death in the rigidity of social and political forms, in the fixity of institutional attitudes and practices — all that prolongs the outlived and essentially discarded even while the gestures are repeated in a kind of sleepwalking, a stupor of numbed habit. In the arms statistics, in the repetition of treaty terms and agreements, in the rehearsals of presidents and ministers, already there is the speech of death. This is not just the natural death of things that die to restore the living, but a particularly human kind of death: prolonged and tenacious, monotonous in its repeated crisis, and oppressive towards innovation and insight.

I am reminded that we learn to live with terror and dissolution, have in the past, and that at other times mass death, whatever the cause of it — plagues and decimation — was everywhere; human minds contracted before it, and life became a matter of survival above all in a universal demoralization. The possibility of annihilation appears on the scene as the most blatant and odious embodiment of the will to dominance and control that is so evident everywhere, unleashed finally to some extreme event here or elsewhere in the universe.

The event may never happen, but as threat it has the power to coerce and demoralize through continual reiteration of the message of retaliation, doom and extinction, a message in which there is both ignorance and arrogance — the self-glorification of people who mistakenly believe that they have either the power to destroy life entirely, or the means to destroy only half of it and save the other.

Faced with all that seems sheer negativity and opaqueness of mind I, as a poet, have only an earthbound perception of the energies and principles by which life is made possible for us, and a conviction that the basic terms for existence will not be substantially changed by any conceivable reconstruction of geography or rearrangement of peoples and nations. From whatever perspective, we will always look back on this earthly home and to the wilderness that is its original ground and source of all values.

Perhaps because I am older, I see how essential now is that surrender to the world and to the experience it offers us. If the threat of annihilation impinges on my activity as a writer it expresses itself in the realization that what is left to me of time and attention must be used with care and not wasted. Faced with the disappearance of my world, I would do the extreme thing and inhabit that world with a greater intensity and affection, recognizing that in this one life, with its related background, lies all the material I could ever wish for, and far more than I will have time to realize.

In times of extreme peril, confusion and insecurity there seems to be something that we can draw on; and one face of this capacity is a belief in the power and sanity to be found in the creative work. That whatever the poem, the painting, the song appears to be saying in any literal sense, it is part of a language, a communication between ourselves and the world, and without which we as a species have not even the sense and dignity of a grasshopper.

Poetry is not a retreat from this century and its appalling news. Rather, it is means of reconcilation. Life is essentially esthetic in its inclination to order, an innate tendency that is desire. A life given to meditation (which does not imply withdrawal) and of which poetry is representative, offers a steadiness and resistance in the face of all that seems determined to disperse us into incoherence and incomprehension.

Only in this effort to be clear, to seek such meaning as may exist, and to find the approximate expression, is my life justified. And when I look for instruction, the shadow cast on the wall by a tree outside my window may have more to tell me than all the editorials and fictions ever published.

Any reply would for me be unsatisfactory and only a momentary repose. But if, as a consequence of nuclear arms and power, and of all that has come into being as accompaniments of these, my sense of the universe and of our place in it has been added to in some way, then I am to that extent consoled that it is not all as evil as we sometimes think.

I find my images of relief, of grace and hope, in the constant renewal of natural forms, and of which my art is no more than an imitation, imperfect and human. The necessary complement to this is that surprising renewal of perception that from time to time seems to spring out of nothing, though it has its source in all that has gone before. Out of self-created necessity, new thought is possible, new combinations, and there is potential joy in that fresh unfolding.

Finally I don't believe in the extinction of life, not even of human life, no matter what scare stories I am told or can read, no matter what my own fears can sometimes imagine. And I refuse to be made numb, pliable and obedient by a threat continually exercised by people who intend to use that threat as a weapon in itself, whether their intention be willed or involuntary.

And while I would not be coerced into acceptance of mass death, neither will I refuse to face the fact of death in any false proposition of life vs. death maintained by a society whose view of existence provides no comfort beyond the grave nor any effective rite of passage, so that the entire subject cannot be spoken of except with the evasive uneasiness of conventional pieties, or else in tones of horror and negation.

Things die, but that is their fate and purpose. And whether it is the death of an animal in the field, the collapse of an idea or an illusion, or the slow decrepitude of an entire civilization, is perhaps mainly a matter of degree and perspective, though of course too of immediate self-interest.

The worst may happen, or it may not happen. It may turn out to be an event beyond effective control, and we will appear as stricken actors in a story written by an invisible author. But I would prefer that we be in no hurry about moving the engines onstage. Nor would I want to assign to anyone conceivably in power the responsibility for deciding who or what shall live or die.

Meanwhile, there is something, for the moment, to end on. Quoted from the *Acts* of the Apostles, it is the closing statement of Hermann Broch's *The Sleepwalkers*, a novel of our time, that while describing with precision the disintegration of a society, does not leave us without hope. Out of darkness, a void into which all recognizable forms are collapsing, the voice of something persuasive and lasting in the ages-long dream of humanity: "Do thyself no harm! For we are all here!"

Patricia Goedicke

The Reading Club

Is dead serious about this one, having rehearsed it for two
    weeks.
They bring it right into the Odd Fellows Meeting Hall.
Riding the backs of the Trojan Women,
In Euripides' great wake they are swept up,

But the women of the chorus, in black stockings and
    kerchiefs,
Stand up bravely to it, shawled arms thrash
In a foam of hysterical voices shrieking,
Seaweed on the wet flanks of a whale.

For each town has its Cassandra who is a little crazy,
Wed to some mystery or other and therefore painfully
    sensitive,
Wiser than anyone but no one listens to her; these days the
    terror
Reaches its red claws into back ward and living room alike.

For each town has its Andromache who is too young,
With snub nose and children just out of school.
Even she cannot escape it; from the bombed city she is led out
Weeping among the ambulances.

And each community has its tart, its magical false Helen,
Or at least someone who looks like her, in all the makeup she
    can muster,
The gorgeous mask of whatever quick-witted lie will keep her
    alive
At least a little while longer, on the crest of the bloody wave,

That dolorous mountain of wooden ships and water
In whose memory the women bring us this huge gift horse,
This raging animal of a play no one dares look in the eye
For fear of what's hidden there:

Small rag-doll figures toppling over and over,
From every sky-scraper and battlement hurtling,
Men and women both, mere gristle in the teeth of fate.
Out over the sea of the audience our numb faces

Are stunned as Andromache's; locked up there on the
 platform
Inside Euripedes' machine the women sway and struggle
One foot at a time, up the surging ladder
Of grief piled on grief, strophe on antistrophe,

In every century the same; the master tightens the screws,
Heightens the gloss of each bitter scene
And strikes every key; each word rings out
Over our terrified heads like a brass trumpet,

For this gift is an accordion, the biggest and mightiest of all:
As the glittering lacquered box heaves in and out,
Sigh upon sigh, at the topmost pitch a child
Falls through midnight in his frantically pink skin.

As the anguished queen protests, the citizens in the chorus
 wail
louder and louder, the warriors depart
Without a glance backward, these captains of the world's
 death
Enslaved as they are enslavers; in a rain of will-less atoms

Anonymity takes over utterly; as the flaming city falls
On this bare beach, in the drab pinewood hall
The Reading Club packs up to go; scripts, coffee cups,
 black stockings,
Husbands and wives pile into the waiting cars

Just as we expect; life picks up and goes on
But not art: crouched back there like a stalled stallion
Stuffed in its gorgeous music box is the one gift
That will not disappear but waits, but bides its time and
 waits

For the next time we open it, that magical false structure
Inside whose artifice is the lesson, buried alive,
Of the grim machinations of the beautiful that always lead us
To the eternally real lamentations, real sufferings, real cries.

Sharon Olds

The Paths

for Martin Garbus

When we are standing in the parking lot
with a gentle sea rain falling on us
you tell me about your client who has been tortured,
in prison, in Chile, his forearm cut off and you
touch your own arm below the elbow, where the
hair springs up in the salt air and the
rain stands in fine drops like a spider's web.
It burns in me to get close to his arm,
my lips on the scarlet at the end of the stub,
my nose near the long wrinkles of scorch
where the iron has been laid down upon the body,
my breast on the blackened skin as if to
take it back into the realm of the human
but of course there is nothing I can do, I can't nurse it or
take its reddened head deep into my sex,
back into the body. I cannot do
anything. All I can do is
tell about it, say *This is the human, the*
clippers, the iron — and this is the human, the
hand, the milk, all I can do is
point out the two paths, we can go down either.

Mark Johnston

War Movie in Reverse

Holes close to smooth skin
when the shrapnel flashes out.
The shores of burns recede,
and flames leap with their hot metal
back into the bomb that rises,
whole and air-borne again,
with its gathered blast.
Leading the plane perfectly,
the bomb arcs back slowly
through the open gates
and disappears into the waiting belly.
The bombardier lifts
his peering eye from the sight.
Swallowing its wake,
the plane returns to base
with its countermanded mission.
The pilot, irresolute now, faces
his commandant, who marches,
brisk and backward
to the general's lair.
The general takes back the orders.
But into what deep and good and hidden
recess of the will
go his thoughts of not bombing?

Jane Cooper

from Threads: Rosa Luxemburg from Prison

Part I. Wronke, Spring 1917

*You ask what I am reading. Natural science for the most
part; I am studying the distribution of plants and animals.*

A huge white poplar half fills the prison garden.
All the songbirds love that tree best. The young leaves
sticky all over with a white down
shine in the sun like flowers!
But by now the small birds
(May 23rd) are much too busy to sing.
Hens keep their nests, cocks with their beaks full
streak back and forth. Yesterday —
yes, for the first time in almost three weeks
I caught the *zeezeebey!* of a blue tit
shrilling over the wall.
At fourteen I was proud, I pitied my mother
for telling me Solomon understood the gossip of birds.
Now I'm like Solomon, that quick *zeezeebey!*
roused me to the sorrows of bird life

I must be out of sorts, just now I was reading
how in the name of scientific agriculture
we've drained the swamps, chopped down brushwood and
    stumps,
cleared away leaves,
while civilized men (according to Professor Sieber)
drove the Redskins from their feeding grounds
in North America

And they made you talk to Karl
through a grating?
I remember in Warsaw
I was on hunger strike, I could barely stand.
My brother came to see me. They propped me in a cage,
a cage within a cage. (I gripped with both hands
to hold myself upright.) From the outer wires
he peered across as at a zoo. *Where are you?* he asked,
again and again brushing away the tears that clouded his glasses

Jane Cooper

But you make too much of my "equanimity," Sonya.
It is simply my way
when I suffer not to utter a word

Sonyusha, I know I can say this to you, my darling —
You will not promptly accuse me
of treason against socialism. Suppose I am really
not a human being at all but some bird or beast?
I walk up and down my scrap of prison garden
— I'm alone in a field where the grass is humming with bees —
and I feel more at home
than at a party congress. Of course I always
mean to die at my post, in a street fight
or prison. But my first self
belongs to the tomtits more than to our comrades

Still, nature is cruel, not a refuge,
and — you won't mind? — I have to laugh
a little when you ask me, *How can men dare
judge you and Karl?* My little bird,
given the totality of vital forms
through twenty thousand years of civilization,
that's not a reasonable question! Why are there blue tits?
Zeezeebey! but I'm awfully glad there are.
We live in the painfulest moment of evolution,
the very chapter of change, and you have to ask,
What is the meaning of it all? Listen,
one day I found a beetle stunned on its back,
its legs gnawed to stumps by ants; another day
I clambered to free a peacock butterfly
battering half dead inside our bathroom pane.
Locked up myself after six, I lean on the sill.
The sky's like iron, a heavy rain falls, the nightingale
sings in the sycamore as if possessed.
What is the meaning of it all? What is the meaning
of young weeds tufted in the prison wall? young poplar shoots?
underground passages of wasp and wild bee
I try not to shake when I walk? ant highways
straight as the Roman? The wall stones shine with wet,
reddish, bluish — a comfort even on
color-starved wintry days — gray and resurgent green . . .

"Wronke, Spring 1917" is Part I of *Threads: Rosa Luxemburg from Prison*, a poem based on Luxemburg's letters to Sophie Liebknecht, the wife of her friend and co-revolutionary, Karl Liebknecht. Both Rosa Luxemburg and Karl Liebknecht were political prisoners in Germany during WW I. They were released shortly before the Armistice but picked up again by government authorities in January, 1919, interrogated and killed.

Susan Griffin

Prayer for Continuation

1.

There is a record
I wish to make here.
A life.
And not this life alone
but the thread
which keeps shining
like gold floss woven into cloth
which catches your eyes
and you are won over.

Kyrie Eleison
Baruch a toi
Hosana   adonai
Omne Padme   Gloria
Nam Myo-Ho
Renge Kyo
Galan
galancillo.
Do you love
this world?

Where is the point I can enter?
Where is the place I can touch?

Let me tell you
I am so serious
and taking aim
like a woman with a bow
eyes looking silently
at each space between the trees
for movement.

2.

I cannot begin now.
I do not wish to write these numbers

on this page here.
224 warheads destroy
every Soviet city with a population
over 100,000.
But once I begin writing
the figures do not stop.
A 20 megaton
bomb, a firestorm rages over
3,000 acres.
A 1,000 megaton bomb
destroys
California
Nevada, Utah, Oregon,
Puget Sound.
Destroys.
California.

3.

Thirty-seven days from my
fortieth birthday. I have
gone up and down this coast
so many times I could trace
the shape of it for you
with my hands, up
into the high cold trees, down
to warm water and
the sprawling city
where I was
born, 1943.
In that year
while I slept
not entirely wanted
in a still room
behind venetian blinds
somewhere in a foreign language
babies were set on fire.
Their cries did not wake me.
Only I breathed in the dust
of their deaths.

4.

It is my love I hold back
hide
not wanting to be seen
scrawl of hand
writing
don't guess
don't guess at my
passion
a wholly wild and raging
love for this world.

5.

(Home)

If you look in this block
in the North of California
you will find a house
perhaps a century old
with the original wood shingles
dark from years of sun
and fine old joints, the men
who made them are dead, the attic
made into a bedroom now, the
linoleum added in 1955.
Twenty years ago
I lived there, a student
studying the history of
Western Civilization, reading John Milton,
looking out the attic window
at a cement sidewalk
which was before just a
dirt path
and Spanish, and was before
perhaps, a forest or a
meadow, a field,
belonging to the Ohlone
who have all
even their children
even all traces of who they were
perished.

Susan Griffin

6.

This is the world I was born into.
Very young I learned
my mother and my father
had a terrible sorrow.
And very young
I learned this sorrow from them.

7.

The mind is vast
what we know small.
Do you think we are not all
sewn together?
I still argue with her
grit my teeth trying to feel
the pain that riddled her body
the day they told her
she would never walk.
I try to enter her mind
the night she took her own life.

Cells have memory!
I shout to her.
Science gave you
an unnecessary despair.

8.

Nor do they argue
nor do they understand
nor do they know
but still it is so.
And there are structures of
unknowing
we call disbelief.

9.

Every American city
with a population above
25,000
targeted.

138

A bomb with the
explosive power
of 20 million tons of TNT.
80 per cent of all cancers.
How is it,
this woman asks,
the brilliant efforts of
American scientists
have been put
to such destructive uses?

10.

It is not real, they tell us,
this home we long for
but a dream of a place
that never
existed.
But it is so familiar!
And the longing in us is
ourselves.

11.

This is the world I was born into.
I saw the wave and its white curl.
I saw branches coming from trees
like streams from rivers.
And the water poisoned
and the land.
I saw the whale leap out of the water
I saw my child's eyes come out of me
                her first cry.
And the air, the rain acid.

Kyrie Eleison
Baruch a toi
Hosana
Adonai
Do you love the   world?

12.

Suppose she lay down her bow.
And went into
that place
stepping so slowly
so surely

13.

This is what I wanted to tell you.
This is what I wanted to say.
Words come late and dark
near sleep.
She said to me
my head was eating my heart.
And what is good?
What is bad?
The delicacy of transmission.
Old alliances fracture
like the cold branches of a
winter tree.
This is the closest I can get.
The world is washed in space.
It is the words she used
precisely those
and I could not remember them.
Only my conviction.
There was badness and goodness.
One was bad.
The other suffered.
And I wanted to
I wanted to mend her.
She told me the whole story
and I told her what was
good and what was bad,
and this was not what she needed.
You think I am trying
to throw away morality
but I am not.
I am not trying to
throw away caring.
In a dream

I see myself
a handsome man
walking without feeling
into a desert.
I am not like him
yet this dream comes to me
and I feel grief.
Out at the edge of this territory
is a missile.
I know for certain
this weapon is bad.
I do not try to mend her
and this makes me weep
for what she has suffered.

14.

(The Enemy)

I wanted you to be good.
I wanted your judgments.
But all your rules became ash.
Your goodness was like an island.
(Your sainthood *was* the sin.)
Now that you have fallen
I cross the water
wrestle with you
charge you to bless me
watch as you
appear and disappear
become me.

15.

The mind is vast.
A whale blows.
Shall we pitch ourselves into terror?
Shall we come home?
Enter darkness, weep
know the dimension
of absence, the unreachable deep.

16.

How far can they go?
This is my speech
an American speech of whalers
and farmers what my
people did
plain, simple, honed
to the point
how far will they go?
Is there a stopping point?
Everyone knows there is not.

17.

What can we make of this?
Two children held hostage together
in a van
for ten months.
What kind of man?
A girl, born three years ago
in California,
a boy who was born in
and survived Vietnam.

How far?
The children were continually beaten
with a rubber hose
and forced into sexual acts
in exchange for being fed.
I am a woman
who reads this story
in a newspaper.

18.

(Bone Cancer)

You must not let terror overtake you.
It is a bone breaking in the middle of the night.
It is a misspelled word.
It is everything you thought you knew
becoming unknown, the leaves
stripped from the tree,

all the greenness orange and dry,
it is pain past bearable, you must not.
Down the street in the darkness someone young
is dying. The soil, perhaps, under your feet
is poison, the water you drink.
What is this? Be reasonable. Disaster
is always predicted and look
we exist. Humanity had a day of birth,
slow, unreasoned, surprising. Now,
is it possible, is it possible
could this be?

19.

Do we not want
this place
to find it
the body again
hearth, heart.
How is it I can say this
so that you will
see too what I have seen.
After the fires
(after the unspeakable)
there will be no home.
And what of us
will remain in memory?
Nothing?

20.

At least we think of them.
The six million.
We long for them.
Want them to be like they were
before
want the music
their mothers and fathers sang
to pass from our lips.
And we ask
How is it they did not know?

Susan Griffin

21.

Do you think it is right
to despair?
No, no, it is not about
right and wrong.
It is the thread
shining.

22.

Kyrie Eleison
Baruch a toi adonai
Omne Padme
New rules
take the place of the old.
Be Here Now
is the lesson.
But I do not want to be.
I am one hundred years away
into the future.
My heart aches wondering.
Will this old tree grow even bigger?
Will its roots threaten the foundation of
    this house?
Will there be a daughter of a
    daughter of a daughter
    a son? And what is the
look in their eyes? Tell me
what you see there. And
do you like to watch
them as they walk across
fields.

Fields?

Resolves

Michael Daley

Credo

Yes, I know. There is only the Church
of Eros. Billion small hairs. Golden.
Winding to the secret of secrets. And I know
in the vast fallen parts of earth, my faith unrequired,
the red leaf mosses build on twists of stone.

Yet I do not believe — I who have ripened
in Church — I do not believe that the unborn in my blood
chanting whispers to polished remnants
of my parents, are not to speak or name,
not to call earth 'Earth', the self 'Self'.

Is it the death of zero we are planning?
At the orchestra, at intermission, a man weeps
for what will be no more. Passengers in the streets
still ride to work, still read. How can we hold the idea?
It is like metal. How can we not?

Is it conceivable the arsenals will not be used?
Europe and the Americas are quiet pastures.
A hymn of diseased flies.
We are large in our flesh, on the ground.

I have seen the fingers of a woman tear at bedsheets,
the streams of labor along her legs, screams
of incomprehensible words, spittle, her open mouth.
I have seen the world open at the top of the head,
crowned, propelled in pain at birth. I have seen it.

I believe that when the morning star fires into the sky
as from a mirror, the sun is empowered to deliver a message
in code to earth. I believe we are that message.

That our conception of nuclear destruction comes 'secondhand'
is indeed fortunate, although it is at the very root of our
(American) capacity to ignore, as well as to indulge, the question you pose. Nothing is more well-publicized today than the
power for planetary annihilation. At the same time nothing is
more unbelievable — except for those who have witnessed, as
have the 'survivors of the light' in Hiroshima and Nagasaki,
the results of our obsession with victory. As the only people
to have slaughtered civilian populations with a nuclear weapon,
we have gone collectively blind, and have leased to those calm,
steady men in office their stockpiles of weapons, allowed them
their scenarios of yet another winnable war, and have funded
their habitual, covert and conventional wars. Wars that have
not touched all of our lives, wars that let us sleep at night
in America, where war is still enacted only on television.

Try as I may to strictly answer your question, I cannot separate
the nuclear threat from the current grisly barbarities that our
government encourages in El Salvador, Nicaragua, Guatemala,
and lately so horrifically in Beirut. Torture, mass slaughter,
devastation that we won't find on page one of the newspaper are
threats to consciousness, but not to our lives. Occasionally
the use of nuclear weapons in these parts of the world becomes
an issue. Then the threat of annihilation becomes the tool of an
economy dependent on exploitation and obsessed with hem-
ispheric security.

I have no experience to bring to writing about such things.
Nor have I a memory of our first use of the Bomb. All the
heinous crimes of government and military, whether of nuclear
or non-nuclear powers, comes secondhand. So I must imagine, to
write about them. At the same time I am overwhelmed by the
awesome, ignorant beauty of land, and the human beauty that
has taken character from the land. I prefer to describe that
— what I can see — but now and then the thunder of a jet or
some other reminder of a never-to-be-prepared-for nuclear
bomb intrudes on the landscape. More often, however, it is
the screams of dying children, of women raped and disem-
boweled, the strange, terrifying laughter of soldiers, im-
passive white faces of the advisors, the voices of politicians
preoccupied with an inexplicably failed economy that swarm
around me when I try to write. It is difficult to think of

seemingly endless massacres within the consciousness of poetry, or to think of nuclear annihilation, despite that the nuclear threat has lasted all my life and that war and torture in far-off countries are products of ancient knowledge, ancient tools.

Nor can I adequately imagine my own death. Yet perhaps imagining death, on a planetary level, is part of the work of the poet, even, as Levertov suggests, in the daily freedoms of a civilized world. To imagine, let us hope, is to act, and to bring about action in our society. Perhaps we must imagine life as well, to make, as is the mandate from the Greek *poiein*, or to forge, as the old 'apolitical' artificer once said '...in the smithy of my soul the uncreated consciousness of my race...'

Seamus Heaney

The Birthplace

1.

The deal table where he wrote, so small and plain,
the single bed a dream of discipline.
And a flagged kitchen downstairs, its mote-slants
of thick light: the unperturbed, reliable
ghost-life he carried, with no need to invent.
And high trees around the house, breathed upon
day and night by winds as slow as a cart
coming late from market or the stir
a fiddle could make in his reluctant heart.

2.

That day, we were like one
of his troubled pairs, speechless
until he spoke for them,

haunters of silence at noon
in a deep lane that was sexual
with ferns and butterflies,

scared at our hurt,
throat-sick, heat-struck, driven
into the damp-floored wood

where we made an episode
of ourselves, unforgettable,
unmentionable,

and broke out again like cattle
through bushes, wet and raised,
only yards from the house.

3

Everywhere being nowhere,
who can prove
one place more than another?

Seamus Heaney

We come back emptied
to nourish and resist
the words of coming to rest:

birthplace, roofbeam, whitewash,
flagstone, hearth,
like unstacked iron weights

afloat among galaxies.
Still, was it thirty years ago
I read until first light

for the first time, to finish
The Return of the Native?
The corncrake in the aftergrass

verified himself, and I heard
roosters and dogs, the very same
as if he had written them.

The poem I have always cherished in this context is Edwin Muir's "The Horses" which conveys gravely and tenderly a sense of the world emptied and then the world stirring to replenish itself. Yet by now Muir's vision can feel almost too consoling, though its consolations are a true effect of its wisdoms. Muir could trust the memories of his archaic Orcadian culture and weave a minimal shelter out of that remote ghost-life. It struck me that "The Birthplace", which had no intention of being a "nuclear" poem, nevertheless touches upon our inability to trust too far a language of continuity: words, especially hallowed words, can now turn into weightless chimaeras. Yet they remain our truest means of sifting the chances of earth and pledging ourselves to a possible life in a threatened future. The best art continues to find occasions where it is possible to contemplate, without being overwhelmed, man pitted against dread.

Robert Nichols

Restraints Against Political Writing

One would like to make paintings like Goya that do political damage, and also paint beautifully and profoundly. In all writers there is an instinct of rage. The difficulty is that to "write politically" can be taken in several senses.

Leo Marx, friend of F.O. Matthiessen, the critic and author of *The American Renaissance*, has written: ". . the new approach embraced by Matthiessen was, in the broadest sense of the world, political. . . . From the beginning he recognized that the significant interactions between literature and society occur well below the level of a writer's express political ideas, opinions, and institutional affiliations. Politics in this sense begins with assumptions about human nature, society, and even, for that matter, literary form and practise." In dealing with Emerson, Thoreau, Whitman, Hawthorne, and Melville: "All of these writers lent expression to the egalitarian, self-assertive, well-nigh anarchic energy released by the American system, although two of them (Hawthorne and Melville) also recognized the destructive form that energy could take in our ruthless economic individualism." Marx goes on to quote Matthiessen as saying: "I would call myself a christian socialist, except for the stale and reactionary connotations the term has acquired through its current use by European parties."

There is here a painful split. The writer is divided—exists in a state of tension which is not easily resolved, and perhaps should not be.

This is dangerous ground. In approaching the line of overt politics, the writer is doing something he or she will pay for, and not only by risking art and skill.

There is a tradition of writing doing political damage. This goes back to Beaudelaire, Celine, Camus, Genet, and includes many american writers, such as Heller and Vonnegut. Without moralizing or making an overt analysis, the underlying order is laid bare, and the corruption is exposed. The other way has been to show alternatives. This Paul Goodman has done in *Drawing the Line, Utopian Essays and Practical Proposals, Growing Up Absurd,* and in his novel. *The Empire City* (the World...New

York City) is about a group of people living at the edge (Hoboken) who are trying to work out a new society for themselves, though with self-mocking intelligence and despair.

My own feeling is that the novel of exposure, of *nausea*, has already done its work and has become less useful. But the literature of alternatives is not yet here. There are difficulties to grapple with. The climate is not right. Movements of cultural history are baffling. There are unaccountable delays. Sullivan— already a practitioner of "modern architecture" and inventor of the sky-scraper—saw the Greek Revival style settle in like a pall with the 1896 Chicago World's Fair. William Carlos Williams was in despair that his own poetry — which became ordinary plain speech and authentic feeling, a style without which younger poets today cannot breathe — would be delayed for thirty years because of the influence of Eliot. What the world is ready for it is not ready for.

It is easy for Lorca, the poet coming to New York, to give an opinion: "In the belly of the monster." But generally the north american writer, writing within the society, loses perspective; the work is without a critical frame. America is supposed to be a country characterized historically by "exceptionalism": the labor movement fragmented by bigotry and extreme racism, with no organized Left. Latin american writers on the other hand are closer to an organized opposition. *A Hundred Years of Solitude* has a cutting edge. In Europe writers such as Sartre and John Berger have been nourished by ties to a political move- ment. For the italian writer of droll stories, Italo Calvino, there is still the Communist party which, though one no longer takes it seriously, is part of oneself or has been; one has a tragi- comic attitude towards it. At least it can be satirized.

The european writer, whether or not a member of a party, moves fairly easily between literature and political criticism. He or she can at least clarify an intellectual stance, though the work may suffer. As Paul Goodman said, the French need only be brilliant; they don't need to write great books.

In the United States there is a more rigid line of demarcation. The author leaves the articulation of a political position — on which perhaps the work depends — to others.

"INDIVIDUALISM"

Americans are the greatest joiners in the world, but there are inhibitions against joining. The group is suspect until it proves itself (not to be fanatical, "brainwashed"). Collective action has not been a recent literary theme.

There were the heroic days of Dreiser, Norris, even Jack London or Steinbeck, when a man fought barehanded against the Octopus or the Chicago Wheat Pit. The wind has died down for the great protest novels. They are like ships left on the beach.

Political writing has died because of its own abuses, and its fall from fashion — after the 30s and 40s — was deserved. The style (Socialist Realism, Agitprop) became threadbare.

A counter tendency: the psychological novel. With Freud came a deeper interest in the inner exploration. The individual psyche became the locus of fiction. It was here that the real work of literature was being done. What this yields to the novelist in the richness and complexity of character, is lost to the character as political actor.

From Theodor Adorno:
"*Monad.* The individual owes his crystallization to the forms of political economy, particularly those of the urban market. Even as the opponent of the pressure of socialization he remains the latter's most particular product and its likeness . . Within repressive society the individual's emancipation not only benefits but damages him. Freedom from society robs him of the strength for freedom."

Contempt for the social is an old story with us. Hawthorne, after a period of initial enthusiams at Brook Farm (during which he signed his letters The Ploughman), wrote to his sister that "communal living is incompatible with producing literature."

But one wonders what it means for a "movement" to be without a literature?

Robert Nichols

THE TRANSIENCY OF CHARACTER/
"HUMAN NATURE"

Bunyan's *Pilgrim's Progress* is a cry of outrage against Mammon.
Christian is a familiar yeoman, earthy and somewhat preachy.
Sir Having-Greedy, Lord Lechery, Mr. Hold-the-World are
recognizable folk. But the characters are not roundly drawn.
One wonders if the notion "character" is bed-rock or if it under-
goes some change?

In the *Education of Wilhelm Meister* Goethe deals with the
growth in sensibility of a merchant's son. This was the period
of the breakdown of autocracy and mercantilism, the emergence
of liberalism. It was a time when such an individual, as he is
developed and realized in the novel, was the motor of history.
This consonance doesn't exist today. There may be heroes who
are thieves, hipsters and even ordinary sensual men but they
are politically marginal.

The situation that exists today is one in which the person
counts for very little, and the system is controlling. This presents
difficulties: can market relations be dramatized, "the invisible
hand"? The comments of Paul Goodman (in an interview on
his novel, *The Empire City*) are pertinent:

> P.G. . . The problem there is to find out something
> that Horatio can fight with. The fact is that growing
> up absurd really is the thing that he would fight with,
> but I don't have it as a dramatic scene. It's clear that
> he can't find a tangible enemy, but as a matter of fact
> the organized system is the enemy, the intangible
> enemy. You can't write a novel, you know, about an
> intangible enemy . . .
>
> M.G. (interviewer) Does society have yet to create
> this antagonist?
>
> P.G. No, no, the antagonist is there, but what I can't
> see is how to get at the society. It's that he can't
> think of the thing . .
>
> M.G. By the organized system do you mean a character
> that personifies it?
>
> P.G. No, not personifies it, no, that is no good. No,
> it's got to be the real thing.

How is this to be done?

In the anti-utopian novel (Orwell's *1984*) the system is naked and omnipresent. Big Brother looks down from the television screen. The central drama is detoxification. The struggle is to shake one's mind clear, like one drugged, and to try to recall a world in which there was a common society and what it was like to be ordinarily human. Simply to remember is an act of resistance.

The swedish poet, Tranströmer, is interesting here. The poet is not (the individual) Tranströmer in effusion. These poems are everyone's biography. They are about shades of feeling below the surface of everyday existence, a person's inner longings and needs.

"I got sleepy while driving and pulled in under a tree at the side of the road. Rolled up in the back seat and went to sleep. How long? Hours. Darkness had come. All of a sudden I was awake, and didn't know who I was... After a long while my life comes back to me. My name comes to me like an angel..."
(translated by Robert Bly)

Tranströmer has been criticized in certain circles on the grounds that any individual is a product of this world (its class relations and so forth). The world is not "given" but provided — or at least defined by those with an over-riding interest. Perhaps these objections are not fair. But in a world where art is increasingly bought — and a Bach program comes to us courtesy of Exxon — it is well to make oneself clear. There is a sky ... there is an ocean ... which are no longer part of nature. From Harry Martinson, another swedish poet, also translated by Bly:

We fished up the Atlantic Cable one day between the
                    Barbados and the Tortugas,
held up our lanterns
and put some rubber over the wound in its back,
latitude 15 degrees north, longitude 61 degrees west,
When we laid our ear down to the gnawed place
we could hear something humming inside the cable.

"It's some millionaires in Montreal and St. John
talking over the price of Cuban sugar, and ways to
reduce our wages," one of us said.

Robert Nichols

In fact poets are more easily political these days than novelists. American poets do not follow traditional images indiscriminately. As Philip Whalen, Diane DiPrima and Gary Snyder know, to write a poem about the sea, and about whales, is possibly to write the last poem about whales.

Poets have kept their moral stance . . voice, and righteousness. And the "open field" technique (of Pound), the loose form, allows room to criticize Usury. There may be little attempt at rationalizing, the connectives are dropped, the line is exact and comparative, a spark-gap for thought.

WRITERLY CONSIDERATIONS

The writer insists on a human nature that endures — though it may not endure. And on a nature he or she sees as threatened. How problematical this has become: *"the space-ship earth."*

There is a tradition of trained excellence, conventions and methods by which writers work, which release their talents, but which now may be a hindrance.

There are many currents in the stream of literature. In time they are infinite. But ours exerts its pull.

It is as if there are three different persons with three different texts or voices. Or perhaps it's the same person, with three voices. The elegant author and the radical critic may join in marches or even help organize the resistance, alongside the political activist. But the activist reads non-fiction and science fiction. "Good literature" no longer says anything to one who wants to know about the technology and financing of power plants.

Authenticity. I am sitting down at my desk. I'm trying to put myself *there.* My first instinct is to get inside the character. Getting inside the character means personally to see through his or her eyes and ears. What I am after is to make a character true to his or her range of possible experiences within the story. The experience is "felt." It is "authentic."

There is one center of perception. Possibly several that intersect to make the story. But it is hard to get outside these, to some world. The focus, the arena of perceptions is narrow. In any case it is mine. What I am supposed to be a specialist of — as a lawyer is a specialist in law — is my authentic experience.

The present. I put myself in the scene. If I am in the right mood I can get into it, get *with it.* The writer is inside the taxi, with Lady Brett and the elusive narrator (Hemingway). She is wearing a certain kind of perfume. Paris ... blurred lights of cafes ... streetlights ... The movement of the taxi through the night. I brush against Brett . . .

Or the moment is extended endlessly, as in Kerouac's *On The Road.*

I am describing normal writerly practise, how any good writer writes, and how I myself try to write as I am writing.

I am after the immediacy of the storyteller's experience ... its flesh, texture. We are moving through it. The paragraph becomes the taxi of "Now".

The writer can be no longer innocent, though the authors of *The Sun Also Rises* and *On The Road* could be. There are too many vantage points; they clash. The preoccupation of the lovers with themselves (the american expatriates in the taxi) slides, with the algerian immigrant watching them as he rummages through a garbage can on the curb. Their experience doesn't encompass enough; this is threatening. Kerouac's wild road goes by Rocky Flats, where the plutonium triggers for the H-bomb are made. For the landscape outside the window there is tyranny in this center of perception, in the illusion of a single Now.

There is a tradition in the East that tries to include space. In his tales the japanese writer Kawabata enters the room, the scene, then almost immediately goes out of it, back to an event or conversation in the past, a glimpse of biography, a sexual hint, a leap forward. All this is tender realism but the perspective is skewed. John Berger tries to make himself — the writer of *G.*, of *Pig Earth* — clear at the beginning: "Take guard." In the theater one of Brecht's principles was to break the illusion created on the stage. "This is not real. Don't be fooled!" With his "distancing effect" Brecht is shouting at the audience to *think.*

INEVITABILITY

What we have to ask now is not: Is it right or wrong? But *MUST* it be so? How is it possible that we've gotten to this point?

Robert Nichols

In recent literature a novel that embodies the theme of
inevitability and determinism is Pynchon's *Gravity's Rainbow*.
In a thousand pages which are sustained poetry of a stylistic
and intellectual brilliance, in which events of the past fifty years
pass in review with characters from a dozen nationalities, the
author shows the events leading up to the Last Apocalypse,
portrayed (with one of the principal characters, the lover of the
engineer, in the nose-cone) by the launching of the German
S.S.I rocket in World War II. An enterprise in which the
beauties of science converge and the entire economic system —
I.G. Farbenindustrie, etc. — collaborates. And to which the
individuals involved acquiesce and which they willed, either
consciously or unconsciously for a variety of reasons: sexual,
psychological, etc.

A russian critic writing about Rabelais said that the novel is
essentially subversive. But the opposite may be true: the novel
is the creation of a leisured solitary writer whose resistance is
gone. It may be now that to describe, to analyze, is simply to
reinforce, and the present novel has become collaborative. It is
precisely the fatefulness of *Gravity's Rainbow*, this pull of the
inert.

Modern experimental forms — from the structuralism of
comparative anthropology and linguistics — may be seen as an
attempt to gain distance from the *reality* transformed into text.
Now literature is self-critical; we look for clues, weaknesses, fis-
sures. What has been called "civilization" is an artifact.

I used the image of the room, the moving taxi, etc., in
"Writerly Considerations" to suggest the grip of immediacy,
texture, the manufactured Now. The "privileged subject"
(Barthes). The totalitarianism of the Present (Marcuse).

If literature is a fabrication . . . Good. Then we are free to
fabricate. This is the point of a book of essays by William
Gass. In it he has something on Robert Coover:

"Before us we have several stacks of unread cards . .
Most of the fictions in Robert Coover's remarkable new
volume are solitaires—sparkling, many-faceted. Sharply
drawn and brightly painted paragraphs are arranged like
pasteboards in ascending or descending scales of alter-
nating colors to compose the story, and the impression
that we might scoop them all up and reshuffle, altering
not the elements but the order of the rules of play, is

deliberate. We are led to feel that a single fable may have various versions: narrative time may be disrupted (the ten played before the nine), or the same space occupied by different eyes (jack of hearts or jack of diamonds), fantasy may fall on fact, lust overnumber love, cliche cover consternation. The characters are highly stylized like the face cards. We've had them in our hands before . . . Just like the figures in old fairy tales and fables, we are constantly coming to forks in their road (always fateful), except here we take all of them, and our simultaneous journeys are simultaneous stories, yet in different genres, sometimes different styles, as if fantasy, romance and reality, nightmare and daydream, were fingers on the same hand."

The avant-garde cannot be experimental in every way. In form only it is showing us the "deck of cards". The subject matter is neutral, often reactionary.

In Barthelme's story called "Capitalism" the middle-class protagonist sits in his living room gossiping and caressing his mistress's buttocks. He looks out the window at "capitalism" — which is like smog, like the weather. The message reinforces, argues for the omnipresence of capitalism (or socialism), for the complete rationalization of the system. But the style explodes coherence.

Ponge, the prose poet, is confident that in writing about The Oyster, and returning to the "density" of La Fontaine, he is being more revolutionary than Aragon who — though the head of the party cell of which Ponge is a member — writes only "band music".

REFRAIN

Everything is balance, of the contraries. The bridge stands. The resonances destroy the maker.

FICTION AND NON-FICTION

Regarding the sperm whale's head as a solid oblong, you may, on an inclined plane, sideways divide it into two quoins, whereof the lower is the bony structure,

forming the cranium and jaws, and the upper an
unctuous mass wholly free from bones. . . At the
middle of the forehead horizontally subdivide this
upper quoin, and then you have two almost equal
parts. . .

The lower subdivided part, called the junk, is one
immense honey-comb of oil. The upper part, known as
the Case, may be regarded as the great Heidelberg
Tun of the Sperm Whale . . contains by far the most
precious of all his oily vintages; namely, the highly
prized spermaceti, in its absolutely pure, limpid, and
odoriferous state . . .

Since — as has been elsewhere set forth — the head
embraces one third of the whole length of the creature,
then setting that length down at eighty feet for a
good-sized whale, you have more than twenty-six feet
for the depth of the tun, when it is lengthwise
hoisted up and down against the ship's side.

As in decapitating the whale, the operator's instrument is brought close to the spot ... etc.

This is the bulk of chapter 77 of Melville's *Moby Dick*, called
"The Great Heidelberg Tun". But was he writing fiction or
non-fiction?

It has always been hard for me to recognize the distinction between Fiction and Non-fiction. Is that my idiosyncrasy?
My hard-facts New England background mixed with a Breton
mysticism? I am inclined to poetry and lyricism but would
prefer to see it in dry things — the drier the better.

I see that, emphasizing the objective side of Melville's
chapter, I have left out: ". . . though in life [this spermaceti]
remains perfectly fluid, yet, upon exposure to the air, after
death, it soon begins to concrete; sending forth beautiful
crystalline shoots, as when the first thin delicate ice is just
forming on water." This is poetry. Towards the end of an exact
and tedious description of the Try-works where the blubber is
boiled: "But that darkness [of the surrounding sea] was licked
up by the fierce flames . . as with the famed Greek fire.
The burning ship drove on, as if remorselessly commissioned
to some vengeful deed." This comes close to politics, the image
of the whaling ship — as the Confidence Man would be for
the later Melville — being the image of capitalism.

In fact there are reasons why the distinction between Fiction and Non-fiction should not be absolutely made, though it is generally useful and in any case absolutely reinforced by the publishing business. Still, we see there is a loss of power to both modes. Non-fiction — articles, essays, abstracts, position papers — cannot really *think* without fiction. Thought needs the person and the scene, that is, the specific in time, to make it supple and to make it tough, otherwise it slides over the surfaces as if oiled.

On the other hand Fiction, when it becomes entirely itself, is weakened through the loss of authority.

I don't mean that it is without truth. (It is by definition fictitious.) It is without the speed, compactness, pointedness that the marshalling of the facts gives. But mostly it is without expert testimony. In the old days Melville had to go to sea to write about the whaling industry. Since Melville's time, work has been done in special fields, scientific and expert. This is how we normally get our information in the modern world. In order to "be original" and to create out of my experience and imagination (the writer is a specialist in feeling and imagination) I cannot use the material for what it is (it is someone else's) but must disguise it as mine. I must fictionalize it.

Does one call John Hersey's articles in *The New Yorker* in the early 50s on the bombing of Hiroshima non-fiction? Good reporting? This is also literature and political writing. This account has entered every writer's consciousness and is behind what is felt. In the same way the "art" of the documentary photograph of the mushroom cloud over the atomic test sites: behind whose retina does not this exist with the searing and terrifying beauty of Goya?

Perhaps for the modern writer, particularly the american writer, "literature" and "non-fiction" would converge in the documentary. This has the density of being fact and record. There is a person speaking with the authority of personal experience — which is not the writer's, though the documentary draws the writer out. One cannot merely say "I have presented this. I am here." There must also be an encounter with characters, which enlarges the scope of the writer as narrator. Nonfiction does not take risks such as these. In the literature of the imagination the writer puts him- or her- *self* at risk.

Robert Nichols

So we look at these photographs of people burning in
Hiroshima, whose flesh is rags, or people starving in the Sahel;
and after the first instinct — silence — we have to allow them
to speak through us.

In this way Millen Brand's book *Peace March* makes poems.
It is a record of his walk through Japan in the manner of the
lyrical travel diary.

> JULY 19th
>
> In the outskirts of Fukuoka City,
> a hospital for A-bomb victims.
> Outside it stands a man whom Yosihara
> talks with and brings to me,
> Haruhiko Eguchi.
> Eguchi says he has been two years
> in the hospital. On August 6,
> in Hiroshima, he was only
> nine hundred meters from the hypocenter
> (a half mile) but was by a pond.
> He believes having water near him
> and having the shelter of garden walls
> saved him. He shows me burns behind his ears
> and on his wrists that are swollen still,
> and on his shoulders. I catch the word "dreams."
> Yoshihara says, "He dreams
> always in an atomic situation." Now
> Eguchi covers his wrists and burned shoulders
> as the marchers sympathetically
> crowd around him. They tell him,
> "We want to ban the bomb. . ."

Millen Brand, an old man who wanted to be useful, was
willing to break all the rules.

But how did Millen hear the word "dream"?

Barbara Smith

"Fractious, Kicking, Messy, Free":*
Feminist Writers Confront the Nuclear Abyss

On June 12, 1982 I marched with a group of friends who had been organizing for several months to express our opposition to the threat of nuclear war and to the U.S. government's ever-increasing commitment to military spending versus basic human needs. We were the Necessary Bread Affinity Group and our banner read, "NECESSARY BREAD: THIRD WORLD AND WHITE LESBIANS UNITE." We were ". . .northern black and southern white; Anglo, Jewish, daughters of engineers and domestic workers. . . .first- and tenth-generation Americans, Cuban immigrants, transplanted Chicanas," all Lesbians.¹ We chose the words for our banner carefully because we planned to use it at other demonstrations for years to come.

As we marched we handed out the statement we had drafted which connected the issues of militarism and disarmament to our concerns as feminists and Lesbians, actively opposed to all varieties of oppression. Since many of us are writers, we had also sponsored a poetry reading the night before at a YWCA in the Brooklyn neighborhood where some of us live.

Not surprisingly, the reactions to our banner and our presence, both from onlookers and from other demonstrators ranged from applause to undisguised hostility. (Some readers may be having similar reactions at this very moment.) The one appalling word of course was "Lesbians." We could have left it out and passed by without a ripple, but we chose instead to identify exactly who we are to an anti-nuclear movement that has been notoriously white, homophobic, male-dominated, and class-bound. Hundreds of women joined us throughout the day and there were many other Lesbian and gay contingents, as well as thousands upon thousands of individual Lesbians and gay men, out or not. There were also more people of color than I expected from my participation in anti-war activity during the 1960s and 70s. All of us were there—female, poor, colored, and queer—because we knew that if a bomb drops no one will be safe, not even the rich white man who gives the orders to push the button.

*from June Jordan's "From Sea to Shining Sea"

Barbara Smith

The organizing of the Necessary Bread Affinity Group provides a context for my thinking about the question of how contemporary feminists who are also writers view the anti-nuclear struggle. I do not intend to arrive at a definitive statement of how all feminists view this or any other political issue. I will, however, focus upon the work and ideas of feminists whose politics I share — activist Third World and / or Lesbian and / or working class women — in order to draw some conclusions about how writers like myself confront the nuclear abyss.

At the outset, I must address the assumption that some writers write politically and some do not. Of course there are writers who agree with Toni Cade Bambara that: "A writer, like any other cultural worker, like any other member of the community, ought to try to put her / his skills in the service of the community."[2] There are writers who are fully conscious of and responsible to the political implications of their work. What I question is the deceptive notion that there is such a thing as "pure" art which deals with "universal" themes, untainted by any political concerns whatsoever. All literary art, and other art forms as well, invariably convey the creator's political stance, even if that stance is the typical white-male-élitist one that an artist is above such mundane considerations. The reason that some writers are said to write "protest," for example, while others are said to address "major" and "universal" themes is that those of us who are oppressed write out of our myriad experiences — including our color, sex, class, and culture — and therefore write in critical opposition to the prevailing political system and culture. Those writers who are privileged and therefore uncritical of the very same society, reinforce its politics at every turn. Any Third World feminist critic can pinpoint the politics in the work of so-called mainstream writers. The politics of a Henry James, a T.S. Eliot, a Norman Mailer scream off the page, yet remain invisible to those whose lifestyles, values, and *politics* they support.

A crucial concept for understanding the perspectives delineated here is that of the simultaneity of oppression. Third World feminists, in particular, have worked to analyze and define with great specificity *all* the forces which undermine our lives. Because as women of color we are simultaneously subjected to a range of oppressions, hierarchies of oppression and "primary contradictions" do little to explain our situation or to offer the tools we need to bring about change. In 1977, the

Combahee River Collective, a Black feminist organization in Boston of which I was a founding member, wrote:

> The most general statement of our politics at the present time would be that we are actively committed to struggling against racial, sexual, heterosexual, and class oppression and see as our particular task the development of integrated analysis and practice based upon the fact that the major systems of oppression are interlocking. The synthesis of these oppressions creates the conditions of our lives. [3]

From this perspective militarism and nuclear proliferation can be seen as an inevitable outgrowth of a political system historically hostile to human life, one facet of a continuum of violence against us. Nuclear annihilation is not the sole threat we face, but one of a hundred possible bloody ends. The major difference between a nuclear attack and other attacks is that it would be so unselective. One's religion, age, race, nationality, sex, sexuality, or previous condition of servitude will hardly make a difference. If the holocaust occurs, a lot of "privileged" people will die right along with those of us who have always understood that under this system our days are numbered. Unlike white folks with racial, class, sexual, and heterosexual privilege for whom a nuclear disaster might well be the only threat they would ever encounter to their general security and sense of well-being, we are painfully aware, as Black Lesbian feminist poet Audre Lorde writes: "we were never meant to survive." [4]

Experiencing and understanding the simultaneity of our oppression affects our writing in a variety of ways: the subject matter, style, language, and most significantly the incorporation of political questions in an *integrated* and *concrete* fashion. For us, the realities of oppression are not intellectual or theoretical pursuits, but are woven into the very fabric of our existence and our art.

June Jordan's long poem, "From Sea to Shining Sea" comments, for example, on numerous life-threatening situations including nuclear arms. Her initial image of a distorted "natural order" is a supermarket pyramid of pomegranates, ". . .encapsulated plastic looking. . ." not to be touched or eaten. Jordan goes on to warn the reader: *"This was not a good time to be gay,"* or *"Black"* or *"old"* or *"young,"* ". . .*to be without a*

Barbara Smith

job," or *". . .to have a job," "This was not a good time to be a woman," "This was not a good time to be a pomegranate ripening on a tree."*[5] She follows each assertion with cryptically phrased proofs:

> *This was not a good time to live in Queens*
> Trucks carrying explosive nuclear wastes will
> exit from the Long Island Expressway and then
> travel through residential streets of Queens
> en route to the 59th Street Bridge, and so on.

> *This was not a good time to live in Arkansas*
> Occasional explosions caused by mystery
> nuclear missiles have been cited
> as cause for local alarm, among
> other things.

> *This was not a good time to live in Grand Forks North*
>   *Dakota*
> Given the presence of a United States' nuclear
> missile base in Grand Forks North Dakota
> the non-military residents of the area feel
> that they live only a day to day distance from certain
> annihilation, etcetera.

After a seemingly overwhelming litany of negatives, the poet suddenly declares, "—Wait a minute—", switches directions and concludes with a positive call to resist:

> This is a good time
> This is the best time
> This is the only time to come together

> > > Fractious
> > > Kicking
> > > Spilling
> > > Burly
> > > Whirling
> > > Raucous
> > > Messy

> > > Free

> Exploding like the seeds of a natural disorder.

"From Sea to Shining Sea," exemplifies the integration and concreteness of Third World feminist writing inspired by complex political commitments. Typical of Afro-American literature and life, adversity does not lead to existential despair, but to fighting back.

In the prose poem, "i can tomatoes," Jan Clausen, a white Lesbian feminist places her fear of nuclear obliteration within the familiar context of household work. She writes:

. . .if they wanted to buy me, couldn't i be bought for a strip of good dirt in an unthreatened country?

but there are no unthreatened countries. in Brooklyn, August, last quarter-century i can tomatoes, sweat sliding into the pots. i am like and unlike other women who've done this: my grandmother canning her way through the Depression, my mother hot for any bargain. i'm of the lumpen now, forever jobless; live on unmentionable revenues; have leisure to shop at the Salvation Army on Myrtle, can tomatoes, think the unthinkable.[6]

Clausen creates emotional reference points for comprehending the horror of no more life.

This poet's use of the details of daily living reflects another characteristic of much feminist writing: the creative use of autobiographical material. Perhaps because the substance of women's lives has been so thoroughly denied, particularly as literary subject matter, contemporary women writers have strongly asserted the legitimacy of the "I." This is not the self-aggrandizing "I" of the author-as-hero, but instead the development of personas and situations derived from the writer's specific identity, her position as outsider. The literature of other oppressed groups has likewise sought to reveal the substance of unknown lives. Black writing, for example, encompasses as-told-to slave narratives, authored autobiographies, and the selective use of an autobiographical stance in creative literature.

Women writers have further expanded the use of such materials. Cheryl Clarke, a Black Lesbian feminist, uses narrative and other poetic forms to convey the stories of vivid Black women characters in her book, *Narratives: Poems in the Tradition of Black Women*.[7] Audre Lorde terms her most recent work of prose, *Zami: A New Spelling of My Name*, a "biomythography" because it combines elements of biography, fiction, and myth. [8] Poet Judy Grahn has edited two volumes of *True to Life Adventure Stories*, many of them by working class Lesbians who refuse to be bound by the distinctions between fiction, oral history, and personal narrative. [9] Much of the writing in *This Bridge Called My Back: Writings by Radical Women of Color*, a groundbreaking collection of Third World feminist theory, co-edited by Cherríe Moraga and Gloria Anzaldúa, is solidly based in personal recollection and self-revelation.

In her autobiographical essay, "La Güera," Chicana poet Moraga demonstrates how the naming of herself is both the result of her politics and the motivation to further develop her political understandings:

When I finally lifted the lid to my lesbianism, a profound connection with my mother reawakened in me. It wasn't until I acknowledged and confronted my own lesbianism in the flesh, that my heartfelt identification with and empathy for my mother's oppression—due to being poor, uneducated, and Chicana—was realized. My lesbianism is the avenue through which I have learned the most about silence and oppression, and it continues to be the most tactile reminder to me that we are not free human beings.

You see, one follows the other. I had known for years that I was a lesbian, had felt it in my bones, had ached with the knowledge, gone crazed with the knowledge, wallowed in the silence of it. Silence *is* like starvation. Don't be fooled. It's nothing short of that, and felt most sharply when one has had a full belly most of her life. When we are not physically starving, we have the luxury to realize psychic and emotional starvation. It is from this starvation that other starvations can be recognized—if one is willing to take the risk of making the connection—if one is willing to be responsible to the result of the connection. For me, the connection is an inevitable one.

What I am saying is that the joys of looking like a white girl ain't so great since I realized I could be beaten on the street for being a dyke. If my sister's being beaten because she's Black, it's pretty much the same principle. We're both getting beaten any way you look at it. The connection is blatant; and in the case of my own family, the difference in the privileges attached to looking white instead of brown are merely a generation apart.

In this country, lesbianism is a poverty — as is being brown, as is being a woman, as is being just plain poor. The danger lies in ranking the oppressions. *The danger lies in failing to acknowledge the specificity of the oppression*. The danger lies in attempting to deal with oppression purely from a theoretical base. Without an emotional, heartfelt grappling with the source of our own oppression, without naming the enemy within ourselves and outside of us, no authentic, non-hierarchical connection among oppressed groups can take place.[10]

Simultaneity, integration, the integrity of writing out of one's total self lead to a wholeness of vision, a visceral exploration of what oppression feels like, what we must be responsible for, and how we can move to bring about fundamental change. That there is a specifically Lesbian feminist perspective about a variety of social-political issues, including nuclear destruction, may be surprising to some. Yet this new writing nurtured by the women's movement of the last two decades poses some of the most vital political and ethical questions of this era.[11] Those of us who have experienced poverty in all its forms are not so quick to accept business as usual, not so unwilling to ask unsettling questions. We are also not in the least surprised by the build up of nuclear weapons, the latest cogs in the white-European death machine.

This element of unsurprise comes through most clearly in the writing of women of color, Lesbian and non-Lesbian. People of color, especially women, comprehend white-male values and culture in a way that white men have never remotely understood themselves. We have had to strategize our survival based upon a deep understanding of the aliens who have invaded our lands or who have stolen us from our own countries in order to serve them. As the ruling race-sex-class, the majority of white men have no desire to really know who they are, to acknowledge the work of their minds and hands, to comprehend the disasters they have collectively wrought. If nothing else, comprehending and *feeling* the magnitude of these horrors might undermine their stranglehold on power, their unearned "right" to rule. Whether we call them "ghosts," or "wasicu sica," "gringos," or "Mr. Charlie," we have been on to the white man and his poisonous capacity for ruin, for centuries.[12]

Barbara Smith

A traditional attitude toward evil among Afro-Americans that I believe significantly influences our reactions to the possibility of nuclear obliteration is embodied in two passages from Toni Morrison's novel, *Sula*. She writes:

> In spite of their fear, they reacted to an oppressive oddity, or what they called evil days, with an acceptance that bordered on welcome. Such evil must be avoided, they felt, and precautions must naturally be taken to protect themselves from it. But they let it run its course, fulfill itself, and never invented ways either to alter it, to annihilate it or to prevent its happening again. So also were they with people.
>
> What was taken by outsiders to be slackness, slovenliness or even generosity was in fact a full recognition of the legitimacy of forces other than good ones. They did not believe doctors could heal—for them, none ever had done so. They did not believe death was accidental—life might be, but death was deliberate. They did not believe Nature was ever askew—only inconvenient. Plague and drought were as "natural" as springtime. If milk could curdle, God knows robins could fall. The purpose of evil was to survive it and they determined (without ever knowing they had made up their minds to do it) to survive floods, white people, tuberculosis, famine, and ignorance. They knew anger well but not despair, and they didn't stone sinners for the same reason they didn't commit suicide—it was beneath them.
>
> . . . .
>
> So they laid broomsticks across their doors at night and sprinkled salt on porch steps. But aside from one or two unsuccessful efforts to collect the dust from her footsteps, they did nothing to harm her. As always the black people looked at evil stony-eyed and let it run. [13]

Or as Audre Lorde succinctly puts it, citing a traditional West Indian saying in the opening pages of *Zami*: "'Island women make good wives; whatever happens, they've seen worse.'" Peoples who have been owned, beaten, raped, chased, starved, mass murdered, and otherwise denied know evil intimately and know also how to survive it.

Certainly this comprehension of the role of evil informs Alice Walker's unique statement, "Only Justice Can Stop a Curse," first delivered at an anti-nuke rally in San Francisco in 1982.

Walker begins by repeating a traditional curse-prayer collected by Zora Neale Hurston in the 1920s. She then says that given all the evil white men have done, nuclear death and destruction seem for them a peculiarly fitting end:

> When I have considered the enormity of the white man's crimes against humanity. Against women. Against every living person of color. Against the poor. Against my mother and my father. Against me. . . .When I consider that at this very moment he wishes to take away what little freedom I have died to achieve, through denial of my right to vote. . . . Has already taken away education, medicine, housing and food. . . .That William Shockley is saying at this moment that he will run for the Senate of my country to push his theory that Blacks are genetically inferior and should be sterilized. . . .When I consider that he is, they are, a real and present threat to my life and the life of my daughter, my people, I think—in perfect harmony with my sister of long ago: *Let the earth marinate in poisons. Let the bombs cover the ground like rain. For nothing short of total destruction will ever teach them anything.*[14]

Walker suggests that ". . .this hope for revenge, finally. . .is at the heart of People of Color's resistance to any anti-nuclear movement." Yet she also reasons:

> However, just as the sun shines on the godly and the ungodly alike, so does nuclear radiation. And with this knowledge it becomes increasingly difficult to embrace the thought of extinction purely for the assumed satisfaction of— from the grave—achieving revenge.

She concludes by affirming that she will fight ". . .to protect my home," and if the planet does in fact survive, ". . .only justice to every living thing (and everything is alive) will save humankind." "Only Justice Can Stop a Curse" is a perfect example of how "non-mainstream" writers think about the nuclear threat. Walker's opinions are shaped by an integrated understanding of the workings of a pervasive system of oppression / evil and her vision does not stop short with the mere hope that the world will be saved. Instead she demands that if life continues, people have to start acting right and work to make this planet habitable for everybody.

I am positive that the way that Morrison and Walker conceive
of both evil and hope springs from an African-American value
system and set of spiritual beliefs vastly different from the ones
Euro-Americans have imposed here. Luisah Teish, a Black
feminist writer and seer, describes the initial clash in values
during slavery between Blacks and whites in her essay,
"Women's Spirituality: A Household Act." She writes:

> All West Africans (and I dare say all Africans) believed in
> an animated universe, that is, that all things are alive on
> varying levels of existence [and] that all of Nature—Earth,
> Air, Fire and Water—is sacred and worthy of praise, and
> responsive to human influence through invocation. [15]

Surely such an evolved philosophy must have been incomprehensible to white people who viewed both land and people as
property, as "wilderness" and "savages" to be tamed. Their
arrogant narrowness also clashed with Native American peoples
who likewise were aware that they were a part of Nature, not
her antagonist. The white man thought that by killing us and
pushing us off the land he could kill our beliefs. But we and our
values continue and the old ways fundamentally affect our
approach to every political and ethical question.

In "No Rock Scorns Me As Whore," Chrystos, a Native
American Lesbian, discusses nuclear and environmental destruction in both spiritual and material terms:

> It is clear to me that the use of nuclear power is dangerous
> —as is almost every other aspect of the dominant culture. . .
> *Nothing short of completely altering the whole culture will
> stop it. . .*
> We have lost touch with the sacred   To survive we must
> begin to know sacredness. . .
> I am still in love with the mystery of shadows, wind, bird
> song   The reason that I continue despite many clumsy
> mistakes, is love   My love for humans, or rather my con-
> tinuous attempts to love, have been misdirected   I am not
> wise   However there is no shame when one is foolish with a
> tree   No bird ever called me crazy   No rock scorns me as a
> whore   The earth means exactly what it says   The wind is
> without flattery or lust   Greed is balanced by the hunger
> of all   So I embrace anew, as my childhood spirit did, the
> whispers of a world without words

I realized one day after another nuclear protest, another proposed bill to make a nuclear waste disposal here, that I had no power with those My power rests with a greater being, a silence which goes on behind the uproar I decided that in a nuclear holocaust, for certainly they will be stupid enough to cause one if their history is any example, that I wanted to be planting corn & squash After there will be other beings of some kind They'll still need to eat. . . I will be sad to see the trees & birds on fire Surely they are innocent as none of us has been

With their songs, they know the sacred I am in a circle with that soft, enduring word In it is the wisdom of all peoples Without a deep, deep understanding of the sacredness of life, the fragility of each breath, we are lost The holocaust has already occurred What follows is only the burning brush How my heart aches & cries to write these words I am not as calmly indifferent as I sound I will be screaming no no no more destruction in that last blinding light [16]

Chrystos's evocative language is solidly rooted in the everyday physical and spiritual longings of people. This is poetic-political writing at its best.

I expect that the ancient female and colored connections that Chrystos and other writers make here may be threatening to some, even to those who say they want an end to nuclear terror. They will say we are "too radical," "too emotional," "too polemical," "too queer." Yet if our perspectives are excluded from the work of this most massive of any recent political movement, whatever its triumphs, it will also fail. This like no other moment is the time for genuine coalitions, an imperative that many will also try to ignore.

But we are not waiting. We are our own movement. We march, chant prayers, dream words.

[1] Necessary Bread Affinity Group, "Necessary Bread Disarmament Statement," June, 1982. The statement appeared in a number of women's periodicals including *Off Our Backs* and *Feminist Studies* Vol. 8, No. 3 (Fall, 1982). It will appear in a forthcoming issue of *River Valley Voice*, P.O. Box 1340, Greenfield, MA. 01302).

[2] Bambara, Toni Cade, "What It Is I Think I'm Doing Anyhow," in *The Writer on Her Work*, ed. J. Sternburg, New York and London: W.W. Norton, 1980, p. 167. Bambara's novel, *The Salt Eaters* (New York: Random House, 1980) addresses nuclear and environmental concerns among many other issues affecting the Black community.

Barbara Smith

³ The Combahee River Collective, "A Black Feminist Statement," in *All the Women Are White, All the Blacks Are Men, But Some of Us Are Brave: Black Women's Studies*, eds. Hull, Scott & Smith. Old Westbury: Feminist Press, 1982, p. 13.

⁴ Lorde, Audre, "A Litany For Survival," in *The Black Unicorn*. New York: W.W. Norton, 1978, p. 32.

⁵ Jordan, June, "From Sea to Shining Sea," in *Home Girls: A Black Feminist Anthology*, ed. Smith. Brooklyn, N.Y.: Kitchen Table Press, Box 592, Van Brunt Station, Brooklyn, N.Y. 11215, n.p.

⁶ Clausen, Jan, "i can tomatoes," in *Duration*. New York: Hanging Loose Press, 1983, n.p.

⁷ Clarke, Cheryl, *Narratives: Poems in the Tradition of Black Women*, Brooklyn, N.Y.: Kitchen Table Press, 1983.

⁸ Lorde, Audre, *Zami: A New Spelling of My Name*. Watertown, MA.: Persephone Press, 1982.

⁹ Grahn, Judy, *True to Life Adventure Stories*, Volumes I & II, Trumansburg, N.Y.: Crossing Press, n.d.

¹⁰ Moraga, Cherríe, "La Guera," in *This Bridge Called My Back: Writings by Radical Women of Color*, eds. Moraga & Anzaldúa, Watertown, Ma.: Persephone Press, 1981, pp. 28-29.

¹¹ For a discussion of the ethical vision of Lesbian writing see: Cherríe Moraga and Barbara Smith, "Lesbian Literature: A Third World Feminist Perspective," in *Lesbian Studies: Past, Present, and Future*, ed. M. Cruikshank. Old Westbury: Feminist Press, 1982, pp. 55-65. Other important sources of criticism of Lesbian feminist writing are Jan Clausen's *A Movement of Poets: Thoughts on Poetry and Feminism*. Brooklyn, N.Y.: Long Haul Press (Box 592, Van Brunt Station, Brooklyn, N.Y. 11215), 1982 and the introductions to *Lesbian Poetry: An Anthology*, eds. E. Bulkin & J. Larkin and *Lesbian Fiction: An Anthology*, ed. E. Bulkin both available from Persephone Press.

¹² "Ghosts" is the term that Maxine Hong Kingston uses for white people in *The Woman Warrior*. "Wasicu sica" means terrible white people in the Lakota language. See Barbara Cameron's, "'Gee, You Don't Seem Like An Indian From the Reservation," in *This Bridge Called My Back*, pp. 46-52.

¹³ Morrison, Toni, *Sula*. New York: Bantam, 1973, pp. 77, 78 & 98.

¹⁴ Walker, Alice, "Only Justice Can Stop a Curse," in *Home Girls: A Black Feminist Anthology*.

¹⁵ Teish, Luisah, "Women's Spirituality: A Household Act," in *Home Girls: A Black Feminist Anthology*.

¹⁶ Chrystos, "No Rock Scorns Me As Whore," in *This Bridge Called My Back*, pp. 243-245.

Louise Erdrich

Nuclear Detergent

for Michael Dorris

My Lord! Even for a jail cell this place is misery. Officer I'd think you might at least take *some* pride in a place. Look how oily those pipes are! That sink's coated with grime! And get a load of that mattress all full of peculiar stains. You'll never know what substances done them stains now, but it don't matter. Not if you know the secret of stain removal. Praise the Lord and just look here at what I got in my bag. Just take a look at this, officer, before you incarcerate a handmaiden of the Lord!

See this mattress here? We all know how rust locks in a fabric. They say death and taxes is the only things certain, but they ain't containing rust. Rust is life's third inevitable. It comes like a thief in the night and it don't leave cloth. Rust inhabits the fibers. It's impossible to evict rust, sir, impossible. But just you watch.

This here God-blessed miracle product I keep in my handbag contains an active secret cleaning agent that goes right to work, scientifically unlocking the chemical bond formed on cloth when you come into contact with rust.

It comes in this attractive white can with green lettering.

Wow! W-O-W. Stands for Wonder of the World. This here unimposing can can hold its nozzle up besides the Great Pyramid and the Empire State. I'm going to spray it now. Just watch!

Do you see? Do you see that rust oozing out of that there ticking? And it's harmless to human skin sir, that's right, it's actually good for the skin. Young mothers spray a ten-to-one solution on their baby's bottoms to prevent serious problems in later life. Young teens pat the stuff full strength on their faces to insure a glowing complexion. Mixed in a cream it banishes wrinkles in golden agers.

There is nothing toxic about it. No sir. It is made of chemicals found in everyday drinking water based on certain of your common vegetable salts. Here you are officer, bless you, use it in good health. That'll be three dollars even.

Yes, yes I think I'll be quite comfortable. I see you put me in with another child of God. Pleased to meet you dear. My name's Blossom.

Officer? Yoohoo . . . whenabouts is dinner served?

He says whenever they get around to serving it honey. Guess that's God will.

Like I say dear, my name is Blossom Treadle. *Reverend* Blossom Treadle if you prefer. I am a messenger of the spirit, that's right, and what are you?

Anti-Nuke?

Well they're jailing us all ain't they. That's right, that's what I'm here for too. Anti-Nuke. That's what I have chosen as my life's work. God willing. I go around putting them intercontinental ballistic missiles smack out of commission.

Wait a minute dear. Before you sit down and dirty up this good mattress I spray-cleaned, won't you allow me to demonstrate my remarkable cleaning product on those denim dungarees of yours? Oh these stubborn grass stains you get in the line of passive resistance . . . they're a chore. But not with WOW!

Put your leg out dear. Let me spray this handy green spray button can. I have some WOW! made up in a decorator flowered decanter set, but them are outside in my car trunk. You know, your hair could use a shot too, and those fingernails. Bit to the quick! Here's a helpful hint. Put a dab of WOW! in your next bottle of clear lacquer and paint it on. It doubles as a nail hardener. As for these here split ends . . .

What dear? You're wondering just how I go about demolishing North Dakota's nuclear arsenal? Well now that is a long and complicated story. I mean, if I was to tell it, I would want to start at the beginning to really make it understood. But since, as you say, we ain't got nothing but time here, I'll be glad to say my piece.

The Lord has brought you and me together.

You know girl, there are some things that naturally go together. You and me for instance, dirt and WOW! Or say Cleanliness and Godliness. Those two things fit together as natural as salt and pepper. My husband and me found this out. His name is Reverend Bob.

Reverend Bob Treadle. Don't you tell a soul, but he's still out there free and clear, waiting for me in a local motel, watching color TV on the cable.

It all begun when Bob and me was preaching God's word up and down the Great Plains and selling our miracle substance on the side to finance our rescue of immortal souls. Salvation was in the spray. Whenever times got lean Bob and me would haul out the WOW! and go door to door with our ministry.

So it happened we were driving through the sunflowers. We were having a high old time. I was belting out the hymns, *From Pisgah's Lofty Height*, and he was watching the road, when I looked in my purse and noticed we was flat out broke. Luckily, we came to a sign. Missile City USA, it said, only twelve miles. The place was Ramgun Country, North Dakota, right smack on the missile belt. We thought to ourselves, what better place to rescue souls for immortality than on a direct missile target!

We drove into town, eager for salvation of the spirit, but also well aware that we first had to finance it.

Now it just so happened that on that day everyone was outside. It was a nice summer's day with a festulary atmosphere. The sun beamed down. The clouds hung in the sky like big white scour pads. Children was running here and there, riding bicycles with long plastic streamers in the handles. Dogs was barking. Cats was chasing their own tails.

"Bob," I said, "looks to me like there's something going on here."

He just nodded in his shrewd knowing way.

There was something going on here and we aimed to find out. So we asked a local passing stranger.

"First one's coming through," he said.

He was talking about the missile. This here town, you see, was economically tied to the missile. All the citizens was rigged up in their best that summer day. They was waiting for the army to drag that first missile through their town and hook it up in its underground silo. There was a band sitting on one side on mainstreet. On the other side a wood platform was set up for the bigwigs to address the crowd.

That started me thinking.

I got ideas. I looked around at the crowd. They were ready for action. I thought of our load of WOW!

"Bob honey," I said, "we're going to have our best sales day ever right here in this town."

He looked at me in his wise quizzical way.

"They're ripe as wild plums for the picking," I said. "I'm going to sit down with the dignitaries on the stand."

With my green and white can of WOW! no different in any respect from the one I have in my hand now, I walked up the little rickety platform steps. I took my place amongst the dignitaries sitting on the folding chairs. I had on my summer outfit suit of orange and white polka dots. My hair was like a bright gold glitterdome. Walking up there all made-up, in my orange sandals, I knew I looked respectable. They noticed me right off. The trick was to have self-assurance.

"We are representing General Wilbert Watkins," I told the commander of the local American Legion Pavillion. "I'm Mrs. Watkins and this here is the Reverend Bob Treadle, General Watkin's spiritual advisor during the Korean conflict."

"So pleased," he said.

"We'll be wanting to say a few words," I informed him. Then I got what amounted to an inspiration. "Perhaps the Reverend here could bless that there missile before you cart it out to insure the defensive posture of America."

"Great idea!" he proclaimed.

So we sat down with the dignitaries, waiting for the missile to arrive on its tractor trailer flatbed. It didn't take long. Pretty soon it loomed up moving like a slow float, preceded by the intrepid bosoms of the Ladies Auxiliary and the crotch-held flags of their menfolks whipping brave and free in the prairie wind.

That missile. Why it must have weighed a ton. It was a big shiny lunker of a thing laying there. The tractor chugged and groaned in low gear, dragging it toward the platform.

"Bob," I whispered to the side. "Gird your loins!"

He watched the missile proceeding with the salutorious calm you see in minor government officials. He had that calm look down good. When the missile ground to a halt right next to the platform everybody stood still around it and the mayor of the town arose in his American Legion suit. He made a speech about the ringing virtues of the American people and their way of life, which was to honorably conflagrate their foes.

All the while he spoke, that missile sat before us, so big and curved we couldn't see the band on the other side. The audience was very silent. I could only see they was worked up. They were getting lumps of patriotic fever in their throats. The ladies' bosoms palpitated in their starched white shirtfronts. The flag holders sat empty below the menfolk's belts, like appeals for spare change.

Any moment, my turn would come.

There was applause. Then silence and expectant panting when my name was introduced.

I do have that quality, don't you think dear, of seeming more important than I am by rights?

I stepped up to the podium with my white vinyl purse. I put it on the stand before me. I took out this little can.

"Ladies and gentlemen of the greatest free nation in the land," I said. "My husband was that esteemed fighting warhorse who saw us through both world wars and the Korean conflict before he was killed by a splinter of his own dentalwork. Today, I would like to do one thing for him. That one thing is the thing I did for him all his life.

I was a grade A one-hundred-percent housewife. I believed in the honor of the American home. I kept my General's private residence spotless and I served him daily meals from each of the four food groups. I had the great honor of polishing the General's weapons. I'd wipe down his carbines, his repeating rifles, his M-14. I'd polish them barrels until they shone with dazzling fury. I'd rub them briskly with a cotton cloth until they begged me for mercy.

And now I am begging *your* indulgence folks. I'd like to do something for the General right now.

In my left hand I have a polishing cloth. In my right hand I have the preferred weapons cleaner of nine out of ten U.S. Generals. God rest my husband. He used it on his own zippers and rivets. He used it on his tactical weapons, on the instrument panels, on the nosecones of his cockpits. He never went into battle with a dirty weapon. He killed clean. It is in his memory that I'm going to polish this missile. I pray to God that Wilbert Watkins may look down during this and see me working now.

And listen here! I'm doing this for the reputation of the American public. Do we want to send a streaked and dirty missile over to the Russian populace? Look at this metal casing. It has all the cleaning problems of an entire household. Dish-water spots here, clinging scum, waxy build-up. Folks, it's even got what seems to be a tough old bathtub ring.

So if you'll bear with me, friends, I'm going to proceed with the ritual cleaning at this point. We all believe in cleanliness. If you're interested in purchasing the wonder product it can be had for only three dollars a twelve ounce can! Just stop in down the street, at the black 1971 El Dorado, the one with the Honk If You Love Jesus bumpersticker."

And with that, my dear, I turned to the ICBM missile.

I had no idea, absolutely no blessed idea, what vengeance this secret agent in my common household product was capable of wreaking on the land based missile system.

I aimed the WOW! I pressed the nozzle. I sprayed it. There was a little latch on the side that opened onto something that looked like an electric outlet. I thought I'd polish that up too. I sprayed the WOW! directly into the slot.

Then praise Jesus! Shout His Holy Name! What happened next near stopped my heart. The missile itself, big as a city storm drain, gave a twitch. Then I heard a sort of hiccuping sound deep inside. From that outlet socket there came a thin blast of steam. Gears was grinding. I heard mechanisms come to life. This here ICBM started ticking all through its skin like it contained a truckload of Bulova watches. More steam hissed out. People were yelling. The band scattered, leaving its tubas hooked on fire hydrants and snaredrums in the middle of the sidewalks. The dignitaries were jumping off the platform like rats off a ship. I stood there with my spray can, shocked, unable to move. Then a low threatful whistle rose from the bottom of the tailfin.

I kneeled before it. My brain was frantic. Bob sat in his chair. He was as aware of the situation as myself. If this rig was to blow there would be a big square hole removed from the map of the United States. It would be like a front tooth kicked out of the 54th parallel. Teachers in the other 49 states would pull down their maps tomorrow. They'd take their scissors and clip out North Dakota like a redeemable coupon.

Perhaps they'd cash it in for Puerto Rico.

Otherwise what a bitter confusion there would be over what to do with all them surplus fifty-starred flags. In the past, as America was busting its seams, they'd send their constant supply of outdated flags to the Indians, the very ones who was supplying them state after state. On the Indian reservations they nailed up the flags on the walls to keep out drafts. But the Indians have their own flags now.

In the future, I imagined, gas-masked Minnesotans would bring their children to the North Dakota border to look over the edge.

"When I was young," they'd say, "that there ground was level with us."

But their kids would not believe them looking into the vast blackened pit.

Kneeling there, I thought these things. Then I noticed the ticking stopped. The whistle was not so shrill anymore. I thought I smelled the odor of sweet gardenias. The missile gave a moaning type of sound, like a dog outside the door crying to get in. The little slots on the side emitted a few bursts of hissing steam and I heard a new sound from deep within. It was a sort of slurpy bubbling, then a little ca-chug, like a washing machine that's stuck between its cycles.

The whole thing twitched again. It yawned that kind of yawn that accidently changes into a burp.

And then the whole thing went absolutely dead silent.

The town was just beginning to peep out of the alleys and washtubs when Bob and I got into our car. We drove away with the mysterious feeling that something miraculous had taken place. We didn't know what a miracle it was yet.

Look here honey . . . just a minute . . . maybe this will explain it better than I could. Wait a second I've got the newspaper clipping folded up in my powder compact. Here you go. Read this, and see what you think!

ANTI-NUCLEAR CHAIN REACTION STUMPS SCIENTISTS

— Ramgun County, North Dakota (AP)

At the climax of a celebratory dedication of the first Intercontinental Ballistic Missile to be installed in North Dakota, an unexplained nuclear reaction grounded the weapon for good. Officials from local defense agencies report that an unknown chemical sprayed into a tiny ventilation duct triggered a timing device within the missile itself, starting a chain reaction that may well have been catastrophic.

The unknown chemical produced surprising results within the body of the weapon. Scientists who dismantled the missile after it was brought to the laboratory in Fort Bluebell report that the complex interior mechanism was reduced to a yellowish "chicken fat" substance rich in vitamins and nutrients.

"Although it isn't edible," said Doctor Osco Butt, Director of Defense Research, "its high fat content would make it an excellent lotion for the hands and elbows."

Residents of Ramgun County have reported a high increase in the number of male gypsy moths within the town limits. Scientist speculate that the chain reaction may have released a harmless pheromone, or female moth sex hormone, which attracted the male moths to the area. There is widespread hope that his pheromone, causing the male of the species to copulate with sheer space until exhausted, will bring about the demise of one of the most destructive pests known to human kind.

County Extension Agent Lloyd Bracken also reports that Dutch Elm disease has dramatically decreased in the past two weeks. For the first time in several years, he also states, the incidence of corn root worm infestations have dropped to nil in Ramgun County.

The final and most perplexing by-product of the chemical reaction is "heavy mud". Ramgun citizens report that it takes three diesel tractors to pull a piece of the substance, about the size of a common bathroom scale, fifty feet. Physicists are hopeful that this "heavy mud" may be the final clue explaining several questions they still have about the origin of the universe.

At Fort Bluebell Laboratories, entire staffs are working round-the-clock to explain the phenomenon which could, conceivably, paralyze the nuclear arsenal here and abroad. As yet, they have no clues, but General Lewis Lake assures the American public that "there is no need to worry. Everything is under control."

Now you see dear, Bob and me was never much for taking Judgment Day into our own hands. We figure that's the Lord's department. So it come to us soon after we found what our WOW! had done, that we was doing God's will by spraying these pernicious vessels, by messing up their critical mass, by turning their insides to mush.

I see you're a doubting Thomasina by your smile.

Well look here. Look at my hands. See how smooth they are? You'll have to admit that my face is remarkably seamless for my age. But don't take my example as sole proof dear. Try this stuff which I call *Atomic Balm*. I'm offering it on a strictly trial basis. See here . . . I got a few sample pots made up in a convenient purse size. It's a little more expensive than your other lubricating products, and why not, there *is* some risk involved in the manufacture. In fact, I was just caught trespassing on one of the local missile sites, which is why you and me were fortunate enough to meet up in this jail cell.

Honey, this stuff can grease anything!

A chain-link fence gets all woozy and the links loose their grip when Atomic Balm is applied in sufficient quantity.

Look here, ain't you getting a little hungry? I don't even smell dinner coming yet. I bet you'd like to get on home. My precious Bob is waiting for me at a local motel. Oh honey, I can just see him now with that gleam of mild savagery lurking in his eye. It's a shame to sit around collecting dust.

I'm just gonna dab this here amazing Atomic Balm in the lock and let the grease go to work.

Better step right next to me dear. I'm gonna wait a few more seconds then wiggle this here hairpin in the catch.

There we go. Got all your things?

Now just pretend like everything's official. Pretend like I'm your mother and come to bail you out. Walk forward. Walk along. Why yes, Praise the Lord, of course you can purchase these amazing products. I happen to have this last spray can of WOW! and of course my sample pots with designer color lids. Three dollars. Praise Jesus! We got a special two for one sale going on!

Jim Schley

Return by Water

I.

There are friends of mine
living in Somerville,
no screens on their windows
so every evening moths come in
to whirlpool,
small dolphins
above the sheets.

For years I've struggled
hand tangling hand
for ways to talk with these women,
my mind
tugged from below
as if by trap-lines.
Once I would have tried
to impress them.
Easier at last to be calm
among women who love each other.

But the land is drying up.
Wars stagger on for decades.
From punctured hillsides are sucked
diamonds and yellowcake:
seventy miles deep
a few grains forming,
millenia's compression
in fissured veins.

One woman told me
her dream of alliance:
women and dolphins in counterpoint,
silver prows bounding out
in the deepening half-light.

II.

There are correspondences, easily sensed.
As minutes throb,
suspended short of air:

there are nights, tight as black
rubber hose
around your throats.
Audible cries,
crosshatched knots and buoys
and the slow, furious
drag as ropes follow
weights.

Millions of dolphins
die in the nets.
Others are clubbed
in shallows, left
to watch their own blood
fingering sand, the crimson lagoon
draining gradually
to open sea.

Or lured out for games,
like clever children.
Taught to tag the keels of ships
for mackerel.
No one explains
the dynamite strapped
on their backs,
the way detonators trip off,
the blistering arc:
waters blanched. How the body
will vanish.

III.

Someone stopped her
in the doorway, prodding
blunt against her rib with the gun,
his face blotted out with a scarf.

He took the money, she backed away,

all evening she cried and shook.
She said to me
"I've been here, despising,
long enough."

185

Jim Schley

Fifty million years ago
whales turned,
broke the land's hold
and slipped free.

Lightning smoke, the acid air.
Tonight you hear from far off
a signal,
a sweet curving whistle.

There is a third
passing beside two women, beyond

the beaches.
There, under darker curtains
dipped to the edge of the waves,

textured, unscaling,
tangible sounds flung out
by the mind in water.
Geneologies of longing

reshaped in the channels.
Ferns and soft rust
enveloping
like new skin
the angular
sunken hulls.

IV.

Poisoned, or fallow— those explanations
given me as a boy
for the wreckage of commerce,
the slaughter in sex
which amounted to nothing
but battle.

The television crackled
and lit up our den,
                              villages scorched:
we saw the rooftops skimming by,
dropped canisters
hotter than grease, pillaged
old women
hidden under thatch

or girls caught running
too slow in the fields.

For this I burn and burn.
Where is water for lips
that jar open?

There were dolphins in the river,
glimpsed from patrol boats.
Each soldier on deck
had a moment
to watch them, a chance
to recover, turning back.
As always, we choose.

I saw my way back
from the radar screen,
the ledgers and newspapers,
where horror
is parceled out for review.
I learned to see
the women around me trusting
themselves.

She can tell that I know.
We retreat to the shoreline to watch

strong waves approaching.
Whatever hope we find
is breaking, ordinary
silver, these thousands
of bright fish that rush
over the reef
as it lifts clear into view.

Changed completely.

Marvin Bell

Because People Are Scared:
This Writer in the Nuclear Age

I have written and published poems about World Wars I, II and III, about Viet Nam, about other assorted political and military matters, and about ethics. If it were not the Nuclear Age (and I have known no other), I would still have written them.

In America now, authority derives from power, not from ideals or eloquence. Democracy in action, lacking ethical leadership, substitutes advertising for reasoning.

The writer is still against murder. He doesn't think that he can say it any better than John Donne did: "No man is an island. Each death diminishes me."

However, he foresees nothing but dangerous confusion so long as the issue of disarmament is reduced to reasoning. It's not that reasoning shouldn't work. Rather, there's simply no hope of agreement among a people divided into those who argue, on the one hand, that abortion is murder and, on the other, that a woman should have control over her own body. If great numbers of people cannot see that neither of these arguments is a response to the other, then he questions their ability to reason in concert about anything at all.

Just as the issue of abortion cannot be discussed without reference to ethical principles, science and society's ability to care for children and mothers both, so the issue of disarmament cannot be approached without reference to science, politics and economics.

I find something distasteful in the nervous leap into calls for nuclear disarmament by people (and this includes writers) who treat each other like shit. Too many of them seek publicity and credit for ethical stands. Too many show little regard for children or young people. The American Left has little viability among people of common sense because it has a history of reserving virtue for itself, and of treating politics as one long series of fashionable parties.

Nevertheless, I believe that nuclear disarmament can be advanced by writers. Because people are scared. The privileged of society, which includes most writers, no longer feel safe from the daily carnage faced by others. The Bomb can reach them. The killing that goes on in wars is always abstract to politicians but immediate and emotional to those on the front lines. Hence, there being no rear echelons in nuclear warfare, the issue is becoming immediate and emotional.

When an issue is emotional, poetry gains eloquence. No one poem makes the case by itself—the "Moloch" coda to "Howl," the "Bomb" passages in "Asphodel, that Greeny Flower," and other such examples notwithstanding—but the accumulation of emotional evidence as expressed in all forms of communication, artful or artless. In turn, this emotional evidence will produce irresistible political power.

The poet is a local animal. He must be satisfied to score small observations and reports, building his authority by the force of his mind and his allegiance to truth and clarity. If he frees his creativity in the pursuit of random fictions, he deprives his art of authority. Poetry does not consist of exercises in style and theme. It has content, and its form must be wrung from that content, not the other way around.

If I am to believe that right makes a difference, I must believe also that that poetry which most seeks truth, and disdains, as much as is humanly possible, both convention and mannerism, will make the greatest difference. But the poet must stand for something. In *The Escape into You*, a sequence of 54 poems published in 1971 but long out of print*, I started off a section of political and philosophic poems with the poem, "American Poets." I said there what I thought then and still think.

AMERICAN POETS

Vision doesn't mean anything real
for most of them. They dance
beautifully way out on the thin limbs
at the top of the family tree,
which we have admired for
its solid trunk and unseen roots

we know go back to other countries
where "God help us" was a prayer
one planted like a seed, staking everything
on labor, luck and no concessions.
All of us remember the rains that year
which exhausted the Czar and the Bolsheviks.

*Now reprinted by Atheneum.

189

Hungry, wet, not yet sick of ourselves,
we escaped by parting the waters;
we brought this black bread to live on,
and extra enough for a child.
That bread didn't grow on trees.
We multiplied, but we didn't reproduce.

"American Poets" is followed by "Song of Social Despair,"
and the section ends with poems titled "On Utilitarianism,"
"Getting Lost in Nazi Germany," and "The Children." Since I
have been asked to look again at my writing in this Nuclear Age,
I must say that the progression seems telling. If we cannot agree
on ethical principles, and if we cannot remember the horrors of
history, perhaps we can at least take note of the children.

I am afraid that we are back to the question of individual
responsibility. It is possible to argue that any act is permissible if
sufficient responsibility may be taken. But what is sufficient?
Obviously, the nuclear holocaust we envision outreaches any
possibility of sufficient reason or responsibility.

The facts are too big and too many. We must fight back with
our emotions, our *common* emotions. Only local action will
accumulate and connect. We are not, most of us, in a position
to go national, nor when we leave our neighborhood can we be
certain anymore of our direction, our knowledge or even our
motivation. Somehow, we must know what we feel in the face of
a confusion of facts.

IN AMERICA

these things happen: I am taken
to see a friend
who talks too fast and is now teaching *Moby Dick*
according to jujitsu,
or judo according to Melville:
He says Melville gets you leaning
and lets go, or gets you to pulling
and suddenly advances, retreats
when you respond, and so on. Ok, I
accept that, but then he starts
in on the assassination of
John F. Kennedy as planned by our
government, and he has a collection of
strange deaths at handy times

bizarrely of people who know something.
I know nothing. I want to know
nothing whatsoever. It once
was enough to be standing
on a field of American baseball,
minding my ground balls and business,
when the infielder to my left
shot me the news of what is now known as
The Bay of Pigs, then in progress
but secretly, and certainly
doomed for stupidity, mis-timing,
marsh-landings, and JFK's resolve
to unaccomplish the Agency's *fait accompli*
by refusing air cover. This would crackle
the air waves, but later. Tall tales,
I figured, wrongly,
putting my fist in my glove
for America.
Moby Dick, you damn whale,
I've seen whales.
America, though —
too big to be seen.

Grace Paley

Anxiety

The young fathers are waiting outside the school. What curly heads! Such graceful brown mustaches. They're sitting on their haunches eating pizza and exchanging information. They're waiting for the 3:00 P.M. bell. It's springtime, the season of first looking out the window. I have a window box of greenhouse marigolds. The young fathers can be seen through the ferny leaves.

Grace Paley

The bell rings. The children fall out of school tumbling through the open door. One of the fathers sees his child. A small girl. Is she Chinese? A little. Up u u p, he says and hoists her to his shoulders. U u up says the second father and hoists his little boy. The little boy sits on top of his father's head for a couple of seconds before sliding to his shoulders. Very funny, says the father.

They start off down the street, right under and past my window. The two children are still laughing. They try to whisper a secret. The fathers haven't finished their conversation. The frailer father is a little uncomfortable; his little girl wiggles too much.

Stop it this minute, he says.

Oink, oink, says the little girl.

What'd you say?

Oink oink, she says.

The young father says what! three times. Then he seizes the child, raises her high above his head and sets her hard on her feet.

What'd I do so bad, she says, rubbing her ankle.

Just hold my hand, screams the frail and angry father.

I lean far out the window. Stop! Stop! I cry.

The young father turns, shading his eyes, but sees. What? he says. His friend says, Hey? Who's that? He probably thinks I'm a family friend, a teacher maybe.

Who're you? he says.

I move the pots of marigold aside. Then I'm able to lean on my elbow way out into unshadowed visibility. Once not too long ago the tenements were speckled with women like me in every third window up to the fifth story calling the children from play to receive orders and instruction. This memory enables me to say strictly, Young man I am an older person who feels free because of that to ask questions and give advice.

Oh? he says, laughs with a little embarrassment, says to his friend, Shoot if you will that old grey head. But he's joking I know, because he has established himself, legs apart, hands behind his back, his neck arched to see and hear me out. How old are you, I call. About thirty or so?

Thirty three.

First I want to say you're about a generation ahead of your father in your attitude and behavior towards your child.

Really? Well. Anything else Ma'am?

Son, I said, leaning another two, three dangerous inches toward him. Son, I must tell you that mad men intend to destroy this beautifully made planet. That the imminent murder of our children by these men has got to become a terror and a sorrow to you and starting now it had better interfere with any daily pleasure.

Speech, speech! he shouted.

I waited a minute but he continued to look up. So, I said, I can tell by your general appearance and loping walk that you agree with me.

I do, he said, winking at his friend, but turning a serious face to mine, he said again, Yes, yes, I do.

Well, then, why did you become so angry at that little girl whose future is like a film which suddenly cuts to white, Why did you nearly slam this little doomed person to the ground in your uncontrollable anger?

Let's not go too far, said the young father. We could get depressed. She WAS jumping around on my poor back and hollering Oink, oink.

When were you angriest — when she wiggled and jumped or when she said oink?

He scratched his wonderful head of dark well cut hair. I guess when she said oink.

Have you ever said oink oink. Think carefully. Years ago perhaps?

No. Well maybe. Maybe.

Whom did you refer to in this way?

He laughed. He called to his friend, Hey Ken, this old person's got something. The cops. In a demonstration. Oink, oink, he said, remembering, laughing.

The little girl smiled and said Oink oink.

Shut up, he said.

What do you deduce from this?

That I was angry at Rosie because she was dealing with me as though I was a figure of authority and it's not my thing, never has been, never will be.

I could see his happiness, his nice grin as he remembered this.

So, I continued, since those children are such lovely examples of what may well be the last generation of humankind, why don't you start all over again, right from the school door as though none of this had ever happened.

Thank you, said the young father. Thank you. It would be nice to be a horse, he said, grabbing little Rosie's hand. Come on Rosie let's go. I don't have all day.

U up says the first father U up says the second.

Giddap shout the children and the fathers yell Neigh Neigh as horses do. The children kick their father's horsechests screaming giddap giddap and they gallop wildly westward.

I lean way out to cry once more, Be Careful! Stop! But they've gone too far. Oh anyone would love to be a fierce fast horse carrying a beloved beautiful rider, but they are galloping toward one of the most dangerous street corners in the world. And they may live beyond that trisection across other dangerous avenues.

So I must shut the window after patting the April cooled marigolds with their deep smell of summer. Then I sit in the nice light and wonder how to make sure that they gallop safely home through the airy scary dreams of scientists and the bulky dreams of automakers. I wish I could see just how they sit down at their kitchen tables for a healthy snack (orange juice or milk and cookies) before going out into the new spring afternoon to play.

Maxine Kumin

Shelling Jacobs Cattle Beans

All summer
they grew unseen
in the corn patch
planted to climb on Silver Queen
Butter and Sugar
compete with witch
grass and lamb's-quarters
only to stand naked, old crones,
Mayan, Macedonian
sticks of antiquity
drying alone
after the corn is taken.

I, whose ancestors
put on sackcloth and ashes
for the destruction of the Temple
sit winnowing the beans
on Rosh Hashonah
in the September sun
of New Hampshire.
Each its own example:
a rare bird's egg
cranberry- or blood-flecked
as cool in the hand
as a beach stone
no two exactly alike
yet close as snowflakes.
Each pops out of the dry
husk, the oblong shaft
that held it,
every compartment a tight fit.

I sit on the front stoop
a romantic, thinking
what a centerpiece!
not, what a soup!
layering beans into
their storage jars.
At Pompeii the food
ossified on the table
under strata of ash.
Before that, the Hebrews
stacked bricks
under the Egyptian lash.

Today
in the slums of Lebanon
Semite is set against Semite
with Old Testament fervor.
Bombs go off in Paris,
Damascus, New York,
a network of retaliations.
Where is the God of
my fathers, that I

may pluck Him out of the lineup?
That I may hand back my ticket?

In case we outlast
the winter, in case
when the end comes
ending all matter,
the least gravel
of Jacobs Cattle remain,
let me shell out the lot.
Let me put my faith in the bean.

Minnie Bruce Pratt

Strange Flesh

She stepped into the building, a blue trapezoid,
as shiny as a skink's tail, darker than a sky-blue
egg laid by the paper wasp in cells of its nest,
more like the milky indigo of certain mushrooms.

Some folk would think this blue a fine color
for a man-made building, or the sky, but unnatural
in mushrooms, would say filth out of rotting dirt
should be brown. Beatrice thought of the way
people confused nature with their own ideas,
lived in contraries, but wanted to see things simple.

Any day she could walk out her back door and see
things weren't simple: this morning, in the vacant lot,
the ground was complicated by rotten circles, a stump,
a fallen tree being divided by fungus into particles,
into elemental dirt that smelled cold and alive.

If she didn't turn the ground, break it into rows,
the dirt would transform itself, given a warm spell,
a slow rain, to clumps of mushrooms, brown eggs
ready to hatch, scatter invisible spores to grow,
to decay, to make more dirt, to sprout seeds
like young grasshopper wings, green leaves, sweetgum
to spread, after years, taller than twenty people,
green, red, purple-black against a blue sky.

Standing on that ground, Beatrice couldn't tell beginning
from end, what was dirt, what was blue, what was her.
But inside the tinted glass she felt out of place,
dirty jeans, dirt blackening her fingernails.
She could see no leaves ever blew in on this floor.

She passed by white plastic chairs sitting
like ideas in the lobby. She passed by small cubicles
where old men were teaching young men the forms,
white numbers chalked on blackboards, how
to abstract from the particular instant, how their minds
set them apart from gross matter. They discussed
the sun, the surface of the moon, like property owners,
as they sat in desks, square, narrow,
                                        the kind
she'd hardly fit in when she was at school, pregnant
one year, always the wrong shape. She got
from class to class holding up her head, pretending
to be separate from her swollen stomach that grew
stripes of hair like an animal, that grew and pulled
like it would pull her down.

                        She'd tried to be not
herself, like Manya Sklodovska in her textbook, the Slav,
the foreign woman, who boiled pots of pitch,
stirred eight tons of dull brown ore to isolate

a hidden purity, a white powder, some part of matter
with the power to transmute itself into another world,
immense, perhaps immortal:
                                    the Manya who made herself
into Marie, a Frenchwoman, scientific, whose radium
    glimmered
pale blue in the dark like glowworms in a rotten log:
Marie who had the marrow in her bones burned away
by pure light pulled up out of its dirt.

Was it suicide, Beatrice wondered, if you killed yourself
trying to change from dirty cunt into pure mind?
And who to blame: western civilization?
                                    At twelve
she'd known that breasts were the opposite of thinking,
could have murdered hers for pulling her down.
                                    In school
she got close to mind only because she was white:
everyone knew that thought was white. Like light.
Contrary to body. Bodies were death.
                                    Yet here
she was, and here were her breasts, wary, but prancing slightly
as she walked.

                    Down the hall people circled, repeating
The Human Race Not The Arms Race. They were in wait
for a man who had killed tens of thousands with his mind.
Beyond them Beatrice saw photographs flashing on the wall:
a chain of actions from the year she was born:

> *A bomb fell through air, the pilot veered*
> *up from incandescent light. A puffball*
> *of dust, the button of a mushroom emerged*
> *at ground level, swelled with its own heat,*
> *stalked and spread its cap, released spores*
> *of invisible poison. Buildings imploded.*
> *People fell dead as light sucked air*
> *from their lungs with a roar. Others burned:*
> *clothes melted into dark skin, they lay*
> *charred wood beside the road. Some endured*
> *the instant of time printed on their flesh: a man*

with face shadowed by cherry leaves, a woman
with breast scarred by butterflies from her kimono,
negatives left on the sensitive film of skin.
Children kicked on white sheets, too many
arms and legs, born like beetles or grasshoppers
with tiny heads, shrivelled hearts. Then
a grown woman with folded pubis, no bigger than
the bud of a five-year-old girl, between her thighs.

Horror between her thighs, in her stomach, coming up
breath scorching, withering her lungs, her breasts.
She shouldn't scream, not in public: she wasn't a child.
And it was an orderly demonstration. If she screamed
the woman next to her would walk away: she seemed
unmoved, steadily watching yellow people die,
people of a different color dying in another country.

In the hall, the crowd of white faces, Beatrice hated
her race: and her skin the coat that hid her in a world
where whiteness dropped, radioactive fallout.
                                        She turned
hot with shame, her face, her breasts. Her skin crawled
on her like burning clothes she couldn't pull off.

She was caught in the skin of the little white man
who was nodding through the crowd, head huge as the globe,
father of the bomb. But he wore his skin like a summer suit.

No need to go hear him: he'd sound like her father
on the evening porch, telling stories about fireflies:
that they were the eyes of little black wizened men,
the jigaboos, with hair like women, feet like bears
and scaley grasshopper arms that would grab.
                                        He'd say
Be careful: they'll get you and turn you into them.

Or maybe he'd flash slides like the movies, matinee,
Saturday afternoon: bomb explodes in a desert,
lower life goes wild, giant grasshoppers gnaw down
power lines, electrocute themselves on civilization,
but white hero, heroine press unmutated mouths
together and live.

Then he'd close with a moral,
voice of apocalypse, Sunday morning: how those who know
as beasts naturally, the followers after strange flesh,
the filthy dreamers who despise dominion, would burn,
ashes of Sodom and Gomorrah, wells without water,
trees of withered fruit, twice dead.

                    No need
to go listen to this famous man: no matter what
he said, his voice would promise salvation by skin.

He would never tell her of the years after Hiroshima:
when Navajo women went blind, eyes scarred by hot dust,
uranium waste: when black women by the Savannah drank
water that burned, wells of plutonium: when her mother's
breast began to wither, heavy fruit to be cut off:

that while she was walking barefoot up a sandy creek,
to follow its thread of light into dark green shadows
in the sweetbay thicket, invisible ashes were falling
on her white skin, her unbudded breasts, radium
blown south by prevailing winds.
                    She wondered
if her breast would die like her mother's, skin
to be scarred, made a desert, twice dead, no breast
to bud again.

                  He would never tell her she was both
us and them, that opposites did not have to kill
each other off.
                  She remembered her father killing
wasps with a folded newspaper, the slam of fear:
Get them before they get you: while insects
batted against the screen.
                  In the hall a door shut
behind the scientist. People dropped silent to the floor,
a die-in, crumpled like any heap of defeated bodies.

Beatrice looked at the predictable despair, and left.
She wouldn't just lie down and die: she would act
contrary somehow, like hair, or an angry wasp.

William Stafford

Next Time

Next time what I'd do is look at
the earth before saying anything. I'd stop
just before going into a house
and be an emperor for a minute
and listen better to the wind
⠀⠀⠀or to the air being still.

When anyone talked to me, whether
blame or praise or just passing time,
I'd watch the face, how the mouth
had to work, and see any strain, any
sign of what lifted the voice.

And for all, I'd know more — the earth
bracing itself and soaring, the air
finding every leaf and feather over
forest and water, and for every person
the body glowing inside the clothes
⠀⠀⠀like a light.

The persuasion that all of those around you may be swept away at once — not just one at a time, with adjustments in between — builds a special perceiving of those friends, these days.

⠀⠀⠀Not all of the time by any means, but occasionally, I find myself addressing this feeling of anticipated nostalgia, this feeling of wonderment about everyday places and events and people. I would like to record the opinion that our time has created a sharper, more pervasive, more frequent mood of trying to realize things that pass.

⠀⠀⠀My poem "Next Time" is for me just an example of that way of leaning into the experience of the late Twentieth Century.

Honor Moore

Spuyten Duyvil

The bridge between the Bronx and Manhattan crosses a small body of water which runs between the Hudson and the East River and is called Spuyten Duyvil, Dutch for "the devil's tail."

1.

A computer chip malfunctions. A micro-
scopic switch slips. You cut an apple into

quarters. East of the Urals, a technician
sweats into grey fatigues. In Nevada

a video screen registers activity.
The President carries a briefcase called

the football. His men sit at a small table
or cluster in easy chairs watching a screen

tick with revelation. You adjust your
blinds. I flip a cellar switch. A terrorist

monitors the football. A red light on a red
telephone flashes. The technician cues

his superior. Afternoon in the desert.
Dead of night in the Urals. Rockets

surge from concrete silos like lipsticks sprung
from gargantuan tubes. I have seen bridges

dynamited in 3-D color, mushroom clouds
engorge and shrivel in 4 / 4 time, faces

of children etched with acid to rippling
wound on screens the size of footballs.

So have you. In a cellar where the ceiling is
low, I bump my head, shatter the only source

of light. This cellar was not built air tight,
but I keep firewood here, my water pump, boiler.

2.

I am driving across the bridge
which connects the Bronx to

Manhattan, river blue below, sun
rippling its surprising expanse

and always entering New York
by this route, I love life.

Planes. No, missiles. Or must we
call them warheads? How fast?

Morning: You stand at your kitchen
telephone then drive down the hill.

Or twilight: You bend at a keyboard
moving as you play. Ten minutes

from that place to this. Frozen
expression on the face of

the drunk who wipes my windshield
on the Bowery. I want your

hand. Warheads. You slip an apple,
quarter by quarter, into your mouth.

We never sat facing each other:
What might we make of this love?

3.

Anyone who calls a broken heart
a metaphor hasn't seen the crack

in this sunset, fire clouds parting,
cylindrical beasts roaring

toward us. Do they land? Or do objects
tumble blazing, each from an open

hatch? Sudden light so bright
it brings utter darkness. Sound so loud

it could be silence. I am blind and
I step from my car. My hair is

on fire. It could be an earring
or an orange pinwheel. My hand is

burning. My hair stinks when it
burns. Below this bridge at the tip of

the city is a white sand beach. Did you
know that? Tell me, why don't you

reach for my hand? We are all blind, all
feel heat which mounts so fast

I can't tell if I sweat or shiver.

4.

My hair has burned back to my
scalp and now my skin is

burning off my brain. Flesh melts
down my leg like syrup. We

won't walk to the river. There's
no mirror and my head is too hot

to touch. The birds are
burning. They say cities will melt

like fat. That one has fewer bones.
Breathe? He was just collecting

our quarters. We were dancing. They
told me this would happen: Hot

oceans, thick soot, flat darkness.
I stay awake to speak this:

My fingers have burned to bone and so
have yours. I never wanted a child,

but I saved everything important
so those who came after could learn.

5.

It has not been explained to us that
a computer chip has the shape of

a wafer but is invisible to the
naked eye or that a switch has less

thickness than a capillary or that
the cloud of fire is as fierce and huge as

Niagara Falls. You have chosen
this distance: We will not hear

the terrible news together. When they
tell us we have the power to stop this,

we speak only of our powerlessness
to stop a blizzard in April. There is

nothing more I could have said to you.
You cross the Golden Gate. Planes?

No, missiles. How fast? None of the
children believe they will be

grandparents. Those behind bars will burn
behind bars and I think of flowers. Why

doesn't this scare me as much as losing
love again or not having enough

money? I will break a bone or my bones
will burn. I can't see what's happening

in Nevada. I keep giving them money.
You're not here. My breath

is burning. We must go downstairs, take
hands with the others, speak something.

6.

When they said put your head to the wall,
fold your arms behind your neck, I was

not afraid. Even when I saw the movies,
I wasn't afraid, but I am afraid of

burning, of burning and breaking. When
they say we will burn, I feel knives. When

they say buildings will fly apart, that
I will be crushed by a concrete buttress or

a steel beam, I hear the weeping of
everyone into whose eyes I have been

afraid to look. If men carried knives
in airplanes, this is how it would be:

Airplanes are silver. They fly across the sky
which is blue. One day a hatch falls open,

knives fly down like rain, and we are all cut
and all bleed. What if, day after day,

knives fell from the sky? I would go into my
cellar, hope my roof would repel knives.

Failure of love has brought us to this.

7.

You iron. It could be thunder. They keep
listening to music. Let me tell you, the

difference is the whole city is an
oven which won't go out, and if it could

there would be no one to put it out.
Let me tell you, you will never

see morning again or early spring. Look,
fire sheets down the river like wind

before a hurricane. Listen, it rushes
through city streets like falls down a mountain.

No one will read what you write. No one will
eat what you put on the table. It is not

thunder. There is no time to make amends.
You will not know her as you wished,

and you will never see your face in the
faces of your nieces and nephews.

8.

Peel the apple with a knife.
Eat the apple without peeling it.

Honor Moore

Choose beautiful paper to draw
her head or draw it on a napkin

after dinner. Eat eggs and sausage
and oranges for breakfast

or don't eat. Drink tea or drink
coffee. Call your father to wish him

happy birthday. Use a bandaid when
you scratch your hand on a rose thorn, or

bleed freely into your grandmother's
linen. Plant potatoes as you planned.

Let the candles burn down to stumps
or replace them with new ones.

I have wanted to be free to feel,
to welcome you with flowers,

see your smile time after time.
When the apple limb fell, too heavy

with rain and fruit, I painted its wound
with tar. This year I will fertilize

so the tomatoes have no hardship.
I am not afraid to begin to love or

to keep loving. Even in this fire,
it is not fear I feel but heartbreak.

9.

Because he is afraid and powerful
he lives encircled by water.

We hold her as she dies, turn the chairs
to face each other. We breathe with her

as her child is born, let him
cry in the dark as he mourns her death.

When we don't have what we need,
we use what is nearest. One day he

swims the moat to explore the place
which confuses him. There is food when

he reaches the lit house, and stars
hang from the towering branches

of ancient trees. We must learn to rest
when we are tired. Every morning

the sun rises. Every spring green
returns to the cold climates. Bathe

with her, stand with her in her house
smiling as she shows you the

new wood. If their anger frightens you,
try to understand their grief. If you can't

understand what they say, watch
how they move. It's thunder. She

is young. Tell her the truth. He is near
ninety. Help him cross the street. It's

thunder. Reach for my hand, I will
let you go. It's raining. If you

visit, we will walk down through the fields
and I will show you the river.

Emily Grosholz

Arms and the Muse: Four Poets

Our age needs strategies for naming and addressing violence, particularly the volcano of human murderousness which erupts so often and destroys whole populations.* Such eruptions are born from the complicit fusion of victim and murderer in a process where both try to purge life of its terrible ambiguity by bringing death to the surface. The root question is then, how can we learn to avoid the excesses of sadism and its no less harmful counterpart, submission? How can we put an end to those black periods of human history when, in the words of Yeats, "The best lack all conviction, while the worst / Are full of passionate intensity"?

If we are to stop behaving like haunted animals, body bruised to pleasure soul, flesh exacting its revenge on spirit, we must confront the problem directly despite its terrors, and prepare to confront it for a long time. Poets have an important role to play in the drama of our moral self-education.

Poets should moralize, and they are uniquely fitted to do so. In the first place, they are masters of concrete reflection, the representation of universal patterns in the rich complexity of individual experience, and so combine the gifts of storyteller, historian and philosopher. Morality, like legal justice, requires the harmonizing of abstract principles with the idiosyncracy, unpredictability and finitude of particular human lives. (When this delicate work of harmonizing breaks down, morality may become dogmatic ideology; those who moralize constantly run this risk. And there is another: the moralist should keep holidays of aesthetic playfulness, so as not to sink into (deadly) earnest. We could not endure the seriousness of our situation if we could not sometimes forget about it, or take up a playful detachment towards it.)

Secondly, the stock-in-trade of poets is ambiguity, as William Empson so clearly showed in each of his three books. I would argue that ambiguity is the very tissue of human experience: we are alive, and yet born to die; we hate and fight the people

*I would like to acknowledge two books which were useful to me in writing this essay: Israel Charney's *How Can We Commit the Unthinkable?* (Westview Press, 1982), and Carl Vaught's *The Quest for Wholeness* (SUNY Press, 1982).

we love; our successes are temptations to complacency, our failures inducements to renewed success; our political institutions both foster and oppress. Indeed, we do ourselves most harm when, exhausted by the contradictions of social life, we try to collapse the ambiguity and take refuge in some fixed, one-sided stance. Unalloyed selfless love will save us, we hope, or financial success, or militarism; we can put on the colors of saint or sinner, victim or victimizer, and be done with it.

Thus our moral education should include facing and expressing our two-sided nature, allowing our antipodes to regulate each other so that we don't explode in impatience and frustration. The richly ambiguous language of poetry is an appropriate means for expressing situations where, for example, the hostility of enemies is tempered by a genuine wish not to do harm, or the attachment of lovers kept vivid and alive by a recognition of hostility and resentment. Or, conversely, poetry can unmask the hidden oppositions that disintegrate the erotic idyll, the too-powerful tyranny.

Probably the hardest thing for us to admit in our attempts to be moral is that the violence we most fear lies within all of us already, in the midst of everyday life. The poets who depict violence in its ordinary manifestations help us to recognize and live with it, exploiting its energy, guarding against its dangers, mourning its excesses. And those who, like Neruda or Euripides, paint its bloodiest excesses, let us think and feel through our deep fascination with and revulsion against it. Symbolic representation of events and human possibilities we would so much like to deny affords us the catharsis of pity and terror. Thus we can confront our own destructiveness, and reaffirm our intention to keep it within bounds.

John Balaban spent most of the period from 1967 to 1972 in Vietnam. His first book of poetry, *After Our War* (Lamont Selection of the American Academy of Poets, 1974), and his book of translations *Ca Dao Vietnam: A Bilingual Anthology of Vietnamese Folk Poetry* (Unicorn Press, 1980), address the sufferings of that country during the war, our war, at the symbolic level of language. His practical response was to spend two years working in Vietnam as a field representative for the Committee of Responsibility, identifying war-injured children and trying to secure appropriate medical care for them.

With his latest book of poems, *Blue Mountain* (Unicorn Press, 1982), Balaban turns back again to reflect on the war in

Southeast Asia. His poetic strategy for presenting the things he cannot forget, which we must not forget, is most often a balancing of opposites: at the level of form, paired and opposed stanzas; at the level of content, counterpart images of destruction and peace.

In the poem "Speak, Memory," a book and a lacquered box "which dry warp detonated / —shattered pearl poet, moon and willow pond—," recall days spent in the library in Saigon, whose windows overlooked the zoological garden where the populace came for a little peace and diversion, to forget the war. The poem begins with a quotation from Marvell's "On a Drop of Dew," the soul within the human flower, and concludes,

> At night police tortured men in the bear pits,
> one night a man held out the bag of his own guts,
> which streamed and weighed in his open hands,
> and offered them to a bear. Nearby, that night,
> the moon was caught in willows by the pond,
> shone scattered in droplets on the flat lotus pads,
> each bead bright like the dew in Marvell's rose.

No image of peace is immune to the explosive memory of evil, no image of violence and imprisonment unredeemed by the possibility of freedom. The droplet of dew, of blood, are emblems of the victim's sacrifice and of the human soul, which suffers such degradation and is yet not wholly destroyed.

"In Celebration of Spring", which begins, "Our Asian war is over; others have begun," counters an image in the second stanza,

> In delta swamp in a united Vietnam
> a Marine with a bullfrog for a face,
> rots in equatorial heat. An eel
> slides through the cage of his bared ribs.

by another in the third,

> And today, in the simmer of lyric sunlight,
> the chrysalis pulses in its mushy cocoon,
> under the bark on a gnarled root of an elm.
> In the brilliant creek, a minnow flashes
> delirious with gnats.

Young students play frisbee on university greensward, and the poet uses such images as a good book on which to promise that "as we grow older, we will not grow evil." If we hold both our despair and our renewed hopefulness together in the same vision, we can

swear
by this dazzle that does not wish to leave us —
that we will be keepers of a garden, nonetheless.

The poem "April 30, 1975," when the war finally ended, suggests the link between our pursuit of foreign war and the slow-burning civil war, violent crime, we live with every day. Balaban begins *Blue Mountain* with poems chased out of the sagebrush of the American West, where he hitch-hiked with the aid of a CB, friendly (and hostile) truckers, and his own open sensibility. The fury of American life is accurately evoked, again juxtaposed with moments of meditative stillness, whose emblem is often the moon.

At dawn in Salt Lake City, I heard swallows
chittering below a bridge as light washed the Big
Dipper.

And then ol' Captain Coors was honking with that
Sugarlips
about the cabbie blown away by his fare.

Outside of Reno, I was sitting in a big Peterbilt
when the trucker waved a snubnose at my head.

Just to let me know, you know. He didn't shoot.
But it makes you wonder about the living and the dead.

Balaban also acknowledges his own inner explosiveness in "Deer Kill," "News Update," and "Chasing out the Demons". In the latter, "a bad case," some aspect or familiar of himself, rages in a deserted canyon, driving a dirtbike against sandstone cliffs. At night he is visited by the ghosts of two Indians, who lead his rage away though they terrify and wound him.

He sat up that night by the dark cold water,
wrapped in a blanket, listening to the creek,

213

> breaking his reverie only once
> to cup his hands and draw to his lips
> the moon rocking on the cold water.

Balaban is not afraid to face the deadliness of life because (I think) he feels so strongly the answering courage and resourcefulness in people, the vital pulse of nature which at the right season reveals that "love like water makes the canyons bloom."

> Vergil said the dead like blood,
> but, really, they are tired of blood,
> and hunger most for poetry...

In *The Knife and Other Poems* (Wesleyan University Press, 1980), Richard Tillinghast takes up many of the themes treated by John Balaban, though not always with the same assurance and formal means. Tillinghast's free verse is sometimes well-wrought by his gift of alliteration into a long, sinuous line, but when that gift fails him his line disperses, and so too do his thoughts.

Two of the most successful poems in this collection are dedicated to his brother David. In the title poem, he recalls a fishing trip they made together, where a knife, "the knife I had used to cut a fish open," dropped from his hand into the Spring River.

> the lost thing   *the knife*
> current swift all around it

> and fishblood denser than our blood
> still stuck to the pike-jaw knifeblade
> which carries a shape like the strife of brothers

His brother dives for and rescues it. So the blood-ritual of the hunt unites them, and the knife becomes a symbol of the profound love-hatred that has always joined brothers.

In "Shooting Ducks in South Louisiana," hunting again brings them together:

> Our blood leaped. We stood up and fired—
> and we didn't miss many that day,
> piling the boat between us with mallards.

Their catch feeds "the whole town of Cutoff" afterwards, and the poet makes one of the mallard drakes a totem in the final lines.

> I plucked a purple feather from his dead wing,
> and wore the life of that bird in my hat.

Blood is ambiguous; it defiles the knife, the water in the boat, the hands of the hunters. But true to the bipolarity of symbols, it also purifies when it is spilled in a ceremony that honors the aliveness, the "raucous energy," that has been stopped. Vegetarian or thoughtless patron of hamburger chains, each of us lives in fact by the death of other creatures. Hunters, like farmers, come face to face with the controlled rhythm of violation which sustains us. So this hunting, ceremoniously recorded, seals the two men as blood-brothers with a bond "like the river   old like rain / older than anything that dies can be".

When Tillinghast raises the issue of war, however, his vision falters, as if he could not keep his words focussed on the event long enough to name it. In "Hearing of the End of the War," though one assumes he means the Vietnamese War, he never says so. The poem's speaker, located somewhere in the Rockies, looks out over windy forest thinking thoughts unspecified, and finally attends to the voice of a baby (his own?).

> A new life breathes in the world—
> fragile, radiant,
> unused to the ways of men.

The only relation to war suggested here is dissociation, and the vague fear that children who are raised in such country retreats still risk being shattered in the next "Great Divide." Balaban's "April 30, 1975," in contrast, shows that there is no retreat, though there are respites; only in the midst of turbulent life can we really catch wind of the fragile, radiant omens of peace.

Similarly, in "Today in the Café Trieste," the poet, sitting in his favorite San Francisco café, recalls the death of Mao, the course of Mao's revolution, and his own days as a student revolutionary at Berkeley. The components of a good poem are here: a rich topic, interesting temporal switch-backs, some fine metamorphosing of images, intagli of Chinese poems. So

Mao wrote: "The Mountain Goddess, if she is still there, /
will see the world all changed." But Tillinghast never draws
these elements together, and so avoids the dangerous task of
making moral judgments.

At one point in the poem, he mentions the Dalai Lama,
glimpsed in exile in Delhi. Surrounded by bodyguards, the
deposed leader steps into a taxi.

> "Place on one side,"
>   he says to his visitors,
> "the dogs of this neighborhood —
>   and on the other side, my life.
>   The lives of the dogs are worth more."

Does Tillinghast mention this incident to show that the Chinese
revolution was justified in spite of, or broken and discredited
by, its incursion on Tibet? The poet says merely that the
passions of revolution, now recollected in the tranquillity of the
Café Trieste, seem sometimes admirable, sometimes absurd. At
the end of the poem, he drives out of San Francisco over the
Golden Gate, and notices, among other things, "a Chinese lady
in silk / looking into the vanished sunset." Why does he
mention her? Was she forced out of China by the revolution?
Did she abandon the revolution to seek American affluence?
Is she a phantom who represents the Chinese aestheticism
which led Mao to write poems about revolution and the
Mountain Goddess?

In Balaban's poem "For Mrs. Cam, Whose Name Means
'Printed Silk,'" there is another oriental lady looking at a sunset. But here we know why she is in the poem, for she is
located by the poet's moral authority and sense of history.
Mrs. Cam lived in Hué, "beyond the Pass of Clouds / along
the Perfume River," and left Vietnam for southern California
because the war blew away her home. It is sunset because she
works at a keypunch every day from nine to five to support
her children, and so walks on the beach only at evening,

> marveling at curls broken bare in crushed shells,
> at the sheen and cracks of laved, salted wood,
> at the pearling blues of rock-stuck mussels
>
> all broken, all beautiful, accidents
> which remind you of your life, lost friends
> and pieces of poems which made you whole.

Mrs. Cam's "aestheticism" is part of an heroic attempt both to mourn her dead and the injustice of their destruction, and to find the means to begin again. She studies the things which start from scratch, a pearl, a poem, a life, and perseveres in her ambiguous translation to the country which offered her refuge, and helped to destroy her past.

Dreaming is the everyday expression of the violent contradictions we all harbor. In dreams we picture our ambivalences in multivocal symbols, and enact the little murders and couplings which, for good reasons, we would not really perform. In general, the more we deny the fears and desires which engender a dream, the more disjointed and displaced is its manifest content; but denied impulses are those most likely to tyrannize us, driving us to sickness or unfortunate action. So examining our dreams is a useful exercise in coming to terms with ourselves.

In particular, dream-poems can often reorder and clarify dreams. For poetry not only articulates the abstract structure of a dream, hypothesizes about its latent content, but also remains true to the rich ambiguity of the dream images. While it provides conceptual clarity, it resists the arrogant intention to plumb the dream to its supposed ground. Our perversity and negativity will never be banished, nor the mystery of our profoundest experiences. The arclight of reason and the candlelight of love must find their place within darkness. Plato was wrong about the cave: we never leave it; our life is a terrifying and beautiful shadow-play.

Mary Kinzie's first book, *The Threshold of the Year* (University of Missouri Press, 1982), contains a variety of dream-poems, some with profoundly unsettling scenarios. They often relate to the war between the sexes, which is not surprising; if we love our opposite number best of all, at intervals we will also hate him most intensely. Thus in "The Pains of Sleep" some pirate-like figure, having narrowly escaped the dreamer's golden ax, watches her jump overboard:

> He watches, light mouth
> filled with fluid, as she sinks.
> The coda of the Niebelungs
> whines through the mast and nervous
> stir of plankton in the wake

as her blood-marbled body falls
through slow-motion witnesses of all her life
and far from the blue pity of his gaze
enters, past the ship's glide.

In "Redhead," the dreamer tries to rouse herself from the embrace of a vampire, talking herself out of it in long sentences of painfully involuted syntax. "The Tatooer" reads the dream from the outside, on the body of the woman he had been expecting all his life, "her skin / a wilderness of intercostal / ice on which her sanguine soul / could be engraved in Ryukyu cinnabar".

Master of a beauty that is pain,
he waited for the ivory girl to wake:
his last and lethal muse with history ahead,
whips in her hair, and from her ribs

to find her breasts, two threads of trembling jet
from the titanic spider he'd emblazoned down her back.

The intimacy of lovers includes bitter discord and power plays. Sartre's analysis of love as a vacillation between sadism and masochism is one-sided, but true to the dark side of eros, and woe to the lovers who try to live always in peace. Kinzie is not afraid to plunge into the erotic underworld, for by doing so she is also preparing an escape route, climbing to light again on the other side. Through poetry the woman finds a way both to acknowledge and distance herself from love's embroilments, smile at the high drama of it all, and get ready to love again; the artist reaffirms her ability to bring order out of chaos by her construction of tense, elegant and masterful language.

In "Ghost at Dawn," the nightmare of having a child and losing it, familiar to many women, is presented and unriddled. So the man-child is last in the line of the poem's ghosts, grandfather, father, lover; he is lost and ambiguously recovered at the end.

...he spoke plain to my questions,
stroked my hair (he loved me best of all),
and then he breathed, moving in my fingers
like a scarf, taut, iridescent, real,
and (this the message weaving in the cirrus
of his gaze)
he was not anywhere.

The child does not exist, in fact; but the slender filament of love and grief which engendered him is real.

In "Negatives," the book's central poem, Kinzie relates the perils of dreaming, art and love to the structure of human consciousness. The burden and promise of its structural negativity pervades all aspects of our life, even our sleep.

> ...in the dream
> the place and color are so severed
> from the glancing run of life, they *mean*.

We transcend the world by breaking with it; live face to face with our own certain annihilation; define our identities in opposition to nature and other people. Our concepts and judgments, our symbolic systems, exclude and divide. We exercise our freedom by saying "no" to what exists. Our desire is born of absence and suffering.

Kinzie's figure for consciousness is the photographic negative, which reflects an event but reverses right and left, black and white, and severs the moment from the seamless flux of nature.

> ...the mechanism of the snapshot clock,
> crystal, cog, and gravamen, is caught
>
> in the helpless working negative
> that serves as memory in aftertime
> when time conceals the beat by which it lived...

The photograph pictured a man whom she broke with precisely because he would not admit their separateness. Love's union, it seems, persists only when tempered by a sharp sense of opposition, and of the ultimate possibility of loss. The past moment's revival in the negative is both an enrichment, for it represents a profounder understanding, and an impoverishment, for it testifies to a wholeness which has been broken,

> as though the brilliant dream ran through a stubborn
>   sieve,
> the dawn bled out and final like the figure in a negative.

In the title poem of his last book, *Death Mother and Other Poems* (University of Illinois, 1979), Frederick Morgan wrote: "Death has lived all times in us / and we in her, commingled, / and not to recognize her is / not to recognize ourselves." Indeed,

our existence is a death-in-life, our vitality tinged and punctu-
ated by small deaths, sadness, sickness, the parting of friends
and lovers; a life-in-death, the brilliant interval between
nothing and nothing. We can rise and fall with this alternation,
or deny it, to be shaken down sooner or later by the explosion
of surpressed violence.

His latest collection, *Northbook* (University of Illinois, 1982)
continues to express an unsentimental, bittersweet view of life.
That Morgan began publishing relatively late in life is not
irrelevant here; one must have lived long, confronted and
assimilated the inevitable tragedies of life, in order to write as
he does. It is the inexperienced who dream up utopias, or
succumb to the harshness of life for lack of skill in the arts of
survival.

The title sequence of the book comprises fifteen poems
named after the Norse gods. In the *Iliad*, the immortality of
the Olympians provides the contrasting background against
which the brevity and pain of human life shows up all the
more clearly. But the Norse gods submit to defilement and
dismemberment, and like us they face destruction. Their time
will come to term, though its span is longer than ours; whatever resurrection may come afterwards is no more than a
promise.

Odin is a figure like Prometheus or Adam, who pays for
knowledge with the torment of self-consciousness, and exacts
the same suffering from us. Thus his story is also a theodicy.

> Your tore out your own right eye, father,
> not because it offended you
> but to gain what you thought would be ultimate
>   knowledge
> from the person who sits at the roots of the world.
> That lost eye shines through clear well-water
>
> but in exchange you've found your double,
> a second head to parlay with
> in time's retentive mirror...

Knowledge cuts us off from the bliss of ignorance; it is the
anxiety of freedom, memory and death which, when it becomes
unbearable, leads us to inflict upon others what we fear ourselves.

The power and immediacy of Morgan's Valhalla derives from
his double use of archaic and modern perspectives. His gods

are both abstract projections of our fears and desires, and personifications of nature, dressed in rich imagery. Aegir and Ran, Njord and Jormungard, are linked to the sea, whose glittering surface covers the terror of hidden depths, whose unintelligible complaint is a bass line to the songs we sing at its edge. The brief poem "Ran" is characteristic of Morgan's mythic strategy.

> Severe lady,
> your nets are out.
>
> They are few whom I would bid you spare.

Ran, wife of the sea-god Aegir, is the sea in its destructive aspect, spreading her nets for drowned sailors. But through his apostrophe, the poet suggests that she is also the imaginative agent of his own feelings of revulsion against the folly and cruelty of mankind.

Jormungard, who one day will try to swallow the world, is a clouded anger chewing on its own tail-tip; Aegir's mumblings drown the sophistries of more civilized gods, who argue and drink in his undersea halls. Njord, dispenser of riches, is reduced to the play of sunlight and water, a sheer relation we delight in though it is insubstantial.

> God unconcerned
> half yields himself
> in salt spray of inlets
>
> and all's refined
> to subtle presence
> where, absent, you reside.

The sequence ends with the opposition of Loki, god of fire and destruction, and Balder, god of the summer sun. They are brothers who require each other, as we must live with both. A "difficult love" attaches us to Loki, for he is a source of energy, humor and wisdom, as well as a great danger. He forces upon us the reality of death and hatred,

> while the world on its way to fire
> trembles at the edge of meaning
> as that which sustains it destroys it
> in the frail moment's passing...

Emily Grosholz

Balder we know only in a pale reflection, for he "had to be put aside, so that / the process of things and meanings might be fulfilled." (Meaning, once again, dances on the knife-edge.) When Valhalla goes down in flames, it is promised that Balder will come back transformed, but even then he will lead his dark, blind brother by the hand.

The hard vision that Loki and Balder are inseparable must not lead to despair. The question is, *how* shall these principles go hand in hand? An onomatopoeic family of verbs, "clutch," "clot," "clench," "tense," which Morgan uses throughout his book to signal spiritual danger, provides a clue. When one of the two principles hardens and refuses to give way, the other will reassert itself, with a smashing violence like Thor's hammer. So we should try to live with a fluid alternation between them, using each to contain and modulate the other.

Northbook closes with a fine lyric, "The River," which offers one version of such alternation. (The moral stance I am urging cannot be presented as a complete, universalized system; each person must find his or her unique and irreducible version.) This idyll does not lack its somber moments, inevitable evening, the uneasy voices of rain and dreams, "dark, reflective aisles of / summertime water".

> A voice spoke in the night
>   while the stars moved slowly
> within our dreaming heads.
>
> Not in ancient thunder, not
> in the still, small voice of the Lord,
> but with something like
> the rain's persistent utterance...
>
> Insatiable rain!
>   Our bodies clasped and clasped.
> The weak stars winked out.

Here "clench" changes to "clasp," and night and day, fear and celebration succeed each other in an easy rhythm, as lovers swimming in a river move between sunlight and shadow.

John Elder

Seeing Through the Fire:
Writers in the Nuclear Age

Ice lies beneath the pit of hell. Nuclear conflagration's final effect will be a massive collapse in which evolution's flicker of forms, with its glow of significance and delight, will be extinguished. Through thousands of years, radioactivity will tick on, but heat declining along a steady curve is not the same as warmth. The secret of generating life from death will have been lost.

The frost-death of earth is almost unimaginable. Its truth seems to be reflected, however, in our society's numbness before nuclear peril. Jonathan Schell has written of

> this peculiar failure of response, in which hundreds of millions of people acknowledge the presence of an immediate, unremitting threat to their existence and to the existence of the world they live in but do nothing about it—a failure in which both self-interest and fellow-feeling seem to have died.

The most urgent tasks facing writers today are to communicate our common danger and to invent a vocabulary of response. Schell, in his prophetic book *The Fate of the Earth*, and Gary Snyder, in his poetry's vision of natural wholeness, are the ones whom I have found most helpful in pointing a path away from this precipice of war. Their different approaches define the foci for an elliptical circuit; together they allow for utterance about an evil which, from any one perspective, would be unbearable to contemplate.

In *The Fate of the Earth*, Schell's goal is to make his readers understand our imminent danger; he wants to speak for life in the language of horror. Hiroshima and Nagasaki, the only nuclear explosions for which we have the testimony of survivors, provide him with many of his examples early in the book. Our present arsenals' megatonnage makes those early nuclear devices seem minuscule, but the devastation they caused still provides our closest gauge for the destruction now possible. Jonathan

John Elder

Schell lingers over the harrowing details of Hiroshima in order to generate a saving revulsion in his audience.

> I have intended to piece together an account of the principal consequences of a full-scale holocaust. Such an account, which in its nature must be both technical and gruesome, cannot be other than hateful to dwell on, yet it may be only by descending into this hell in imagination now that we can hope to escape descending into it in reality at some later time.

One of Schell's central affinities as a writer is with Jonathan Edwards, whose sermon "Sinners in the Hands of an Angry God" was constructed to give his congregation a vivid experience of damnation: "That world of misery, that lake of burning brimstone, is extended abroad under you. There is the dreadful pit of the glowing flames of the wrath of God. . . ." Both authors want to arouse their communities out of mortal numbness, to make language an instrument of conversion. But a writer's strategy of emphasizing the worst may overwhelm a reader, deadening the intended effect of a reaction *against* that evil. Schell tries through his book to encourage a crucial transfer of sovereignty, in which nation-states will give way to a global community. Such a political ideal, however, developed in Part III of *The Fate of the Earth*, comes across less forcefully than the horrors which it would help to avoid. Perhaps the problem he faces as a writer is that the fires of Hiroshima possess us as sensations rather than simply as ideas. They are images that scald the mind. Awakening the reader from complacency, they leave a different kind of numbness, that of shock, and mute those other passages that would look *away* from the abyss.

Such tensions are unavoidable in any attempt at education through dread. But there is also a thread of Schell's book that leads towards a possible resolution. It is a refrain that reverberates with Gary Snyder's poetry, and one that both includes and balances the prospect of a nuclear war. Although Schell's general, prophetic emphasis is on the looming destruction of humanity, from time to time he speaks as well to the probable disruption of nature's regenerative cycle. "Extinction is the death of death," he writes, and of earth's sustaining miracle of rebirth through decay. This thread shines through at a number of places in the book, as an ecological vision involving a transfer of sovereignty much more fundamental than a move away from the nation-state. Affirming value in the natural world, beyond all human projects, we may recover a sense of saving reality outside the bounds of our own solutions and designs. "Now reason must sit at the knee of instinct and learn reverence for the miraculous instinctual capacity for creation."

The human species long ago transferred its evolutionary process into the cultural realm. Our physical and mental capabilities have developed increasingly through social specialization and centralized technology. It is obvious that humanity has now arrived at an evolutionary crisis: having learned the trick of setting air on fire, we must now also learn, soon or not at all, to move beyond such fatal technique. Schell's book seeks, by conveying our enormous danger, to arrest civilization's rush toward the brink. The question, though, is where we *can* go, when so much of human evolution's momentum has been directed to this present juncture of aggression and devastating force.

A nation that assumes its right to destroy the world unless certain political purposes are achieved aligns itself with Edwards's angry God, setting itself up as an authority beyond and above the frame of nature. To give up this prerogative we must find a different understanding of nature's connection with the divine. And it is because of such a need that Schell's glimpses of regenerative nature, as both the context and the casualty of nuclear holocaust, become so important. After facing the prospect of nuclear annihilation we must somewhere find the strength to look away, and thus to avoid paralytic terror. Edwards himself felt a need to balance his sermons about hellfire with long walks in the woods near Northampton and Pittsfield; leaving his study, he entered the larger circuit of God's mercy. Nature's process allows for a mediated experience of holy warmth, and supplies a model for relationship that corrects the sublime self-righteousness of the nuclear strategies. Wrath can bring no end to wrath. In our writing, as in our nation's policies, we must give up all claims to sovereignty over the earth.

It would seem a contradiction to discuss our society's nuclear peril simultaneously in religious and in evolutionary terms, were it not for the cultural dimension of humanity's development. Nuclear weapons reflect our technology's accelerating advance, and force a search for purposeful restraint in the face of such

225

power. In the last chapter of *Process and Reality*, Whitehead addresses the West's apocalyptic faith within such an evolutionary perspective. The Judaeo-Christian tradition, he finds, has upheld a series of monolithic Gods, expressing the absolute values—moral, rational, and political, respectively—of the Jewish, Greek, and Roman peoples. Just as a naturalist yearning is intertwined throughout Schell's vision of the last days, however, there is a persistent strain in the Western tradition that runs counter to all religious absolutes. In the psalms and in the parables of Jesus alike, the features of nature form a countenance expressive of mercy. Whitehead writes:

> There is in the Galilean origin of Christianity yet another suggestion which does not fit very well with any of the three main strands of thought. It does not emphasize the ruling Caesar, or the ruthless moralist, or the unmoved mover. It dwells upon the tender elements in the world, which slowly and in quietness operate by love; and it finds purpose in the present immediacy of a kingdom not of this world. Love neither rules nor is it unmoved; also it is a little oblivious as to morals. It does not look to the future; for it finds its own reward in the immediate present.

Whitehead's vision of Galilean tenderness accords well with an ecological response to the nuclear arms race. An understanding of wholeness replaces abstraction and dualism: there is one earth, one cycle of water through its oceans and atmosphere, and through all living things. Such a perspective can recognize the full enormity of nuclear destruction while also providing a source of hope. Becoming aware that we depend upon a larger world, we may gain the humility in which to choose a human order harmonious with the earth. An important term in anger's theology has always been *sin*—the infraction that justifies violent punishment. But the word so translated in the English New Testament is the Greek *hamartia*, which more literally means "non-involvement" or "separation." The opposite of sin, in the light of such an etymology, is not a passive virtue. Rather, it is participation, affirmation of the sustaining world in which "we live and move and have our being."

The value of Jonathan Schell's book is twofold—as a searing evocation of nuclear holocaust, recalling us to our imminent danger, and as an account through which regenerative imagery of nature is dispersed. As I have suggested, *The Fate of the Earth* is, on one important level, a revivalist sermon. Schell brings the scriptures and tradition of the West to bear on the present; he calls on our society to be converted. Gary Snyder develops a very different cultural perspective within his writing, and his principal affinities are with Native American and Buddhist models rather than with the Judaeo-Christian tradition. But in his poem "For Nothing" Snyder speaks to the important implication of Schell's book, the vision of nature as redemptive precisely because it remains outside human design.

> Earth a flower
> A phlox on the steep
> slope of light
> hanging over the vast
> solid spaces
> small rotten crystals;
> salts.
>
> Earth a flower
> by a gulf where a raven
> flaps by once
> a glimmer, a color
> forgotten as all
> falls away.
>
> A flower
> for nothing;
> an offer;
> no taker;
>
> Snow-trickle, feldspar, dirt.

Snyder's poem speaks to the needs and possibilities of our evolutionary moment. In poetry as in politics, we must move beyond the assumption of value separable from the earth. There are certain natural images that arrest the mind and make *possible* such a reorientation. In their integrity and self-enclosure, they allow simultaneously for reflection on the whirling world of process and participation within it. The blue-green ball of earth, marbled with clouds and showing against deep blackness, is such an image of dynamic containment. One of the astronauts who first looked down on earth from orbit wept at its beauty. And the NASA photograph of our planet that has been so widely circulated retains a fascination and emotional impact that no amount of exposure can reduce to a cliche. "For Nothing" holds to this perspective on the earth from space. Where Schell wants to bring the heat of an explosion into his reader's mind, to evoke the magnitude of potential destruction, Snyder's poem takes a cooling step away, so that the *smallness* of our world may be felt.

When Snyder writes of "A phlox on the steep / slopes of light," he echoes the phrase with which John Muir described the Sierra Nevada: "the range of light." A mountain wildflower, its delicacy all the more precious because surrounded by the vastness of dramatic geological forms, draws responses of restraint and quietness from hikers who come upon it. The pink and white of alpine phlox makes you careful where you put your feet; it mutes the talk and laughter of a group, but enhances the spirit of adventure shared. A flower's smallness, revealed against such a slope, is matched by its transience. Blooming in that short period between the melting of snow and the snow-melt's evaporation into dry air, phlox finds its completeness in a moment. Phlox—flame, but only the briefest flicker—vanishing so quickly into the space from which its small order arose. Such beauty evokes a response of longing; even as we see it, we know it is passing away. The gift of Snyder's poem is a recognition of this earth-flower's beauty, too, so often beneath our caring as it is beneath our feet.

"For Nothing" gains in reverberation through its avoidance of closed syntax. By letting images speak beyond the bounds of a single sentence, Snyder approaches the open-ended simplicity of nature. Even his title carries such divergent possibilities. It may express the *waste* of earth's beauty: "an offer / no taker." So much of human history and culture has disregarded earth's delicate harmony, its short achievement of equilibrium. As our nuclear armaments threaten the ecosphere, earth seems also in danger of becoming "a color / forgotten as all / falls away." Jonathan Schell mentions the apparent probability that after a nuclear holocaust the sky would turn brown and opaque. But the words "For Nothing" may speak as well to the *liberating* quality of such beauty for a humanity ensnared in its own heed-lessness: earth, like a wildflower, is beautiful for no purpose beyond itself. It is a world offering only relationship, not any decisive resolution. In this connection, one might see the title in yet another way—as dedication. "Nothingness" can be an escape from hierarchical order, into the freedom of immediacy and particularity.

Part of the liberation in "For Nothing" comes in the fact that, along with definitive syntax, the personal pronoun is left behind. There is a certain detached, "impersonal" quality about the poem that possesses tremendous potential for human meaning. In order to see the earth without the shadows of our projects falling across the slope of light we have to step back, and the astronomical perspective on our planet is one way of achieving such a beneficial distancing. To see earth blooming briefly in reflected light is to gain a new fidelity to it. Schell sets out to arouse in us an anguished awareness of the danger to all terrestrial life, while Snyder proceeds by distancing and detachment. But they complement each other as writers, in a cycle of human response including the discursive and the poetic, the admonitory and the celebratory voices. Perhaps, taken together, they suggest that we need to *act* as if we are respon-sible for the fate of the earth but *feel* as if we are not. Both activism and faith may come from surrender to a larger truth than one can comprehend.

In the last line of "For Nothing," "Snow-trickle, feldspar, dirt," we see the genesis of soil from which the flower of the first line may grow again. We need, it seems from this poem, to take a longer view of the cycle of life, to gain strength for working against nuclear war by becoming *less* impressed with the prospect. The austerity of Snyder's poem allows him to value the rock as well as the flower, the gulf as well as the glimmer beside it. Such an inclusiveness is anti-apocalyptic. It no more allows nuclear holocaust a definitive status than it imposes a closed syntax on the turning earth: eternity may be present in a moment, and in the passage through space of evanescent forms. Vital warmth comes not from an avoidance of either heat or cold, but from a continual capacity for *reacting* to them. Life turns with the earth.

Here in New England, as the days are lengthening into March and the twilight is increasingly prolonged, the sky still holds the clarity of winter. Last night, looking out from Bristol, toward the Adirondacks' silhouette across the Lake, I could watch the colors changing for two hours. Dull rose at the horizon quickly lifted into lemon and blue; an overlay of gray and mauve continued the upward curve, in a much more gradual transition to the zenith's black. Against the darkening sky, the moon was the thinnest of crescents, illuminating the lower right quarter of a disk that would otherwise have been invisible. Venus hung below and to the North, brighter than the moon and white instead of silver. Though the curve might have been taken to close a parenthetical remark and the point to show a proposition's end, there was no sentence in the sky. It was just another chance to look at the sun, reflecting on the moon, diffusing through the atmosphere. Walking out at night, we can remember the morning.

Contributors

Zoe Anglesey's collection *Something More Than Force, Poems for Guatemala, 1971-1982*, was published by Adastra Press; she is from Oregon, living now in New York City. The epigrammatic piece by **W. H. Auden** appears early in his oratorio *For the Time Being*, spoken by the Narrator. **John Balaban** is a poet — author of *After Our War* (University of Pittsburgh Press: Lamont Selection for 1974) and *Blue Mountain* (Unicorn) — as well as a translator from Vietnamese, Bulgarian, and Romanian; he teaches at Penn State. **Marvin Bell**'s latest books of poems are *Drawn by Stones, by Earth, by Things that Have Been in the Fire* (Atheneum) and, with William Stafford, *Segues: A Correspondence in Poetry*, (Godine). **S. Ben-Tov**'s first collection of poems, *During Cease Fire*, will be published by Harper & Row in 1985. **William Carpenter** teaches at College of the Atlantic in Maine, and his book *The Hours of Morning* (Virginia Commonwealth University Press) won an AWP Award. **Amy Clampitt** is author of *The Kingfisher* and the forthcoming *What the Light Was Like*, both from Knopf. **Jane Cooper**'s *Threads: Rosa Luxemburg from Prison* was first published as a Flamingo Press chapbook to benefit the White House Lawn Eleven, an antinuclear group from the War Resisters League; the complete poem is included in *Scaffolding: New and Selected Poems*, from England's Anvil Press, Ltd. **Michael Daley** lives in Port Townsend, Washington. His book *The Straits*, which contains the poem "Credo," was published by Empty Bowl in 1983. A native of the Northwest, **Madeline DeFrees** plans to return in 1985 after several years teaching at the University of Massachusetts; her *Magpie in the Gallows* is available from Copper Canyon Press. **Terrence Des Pres** lives in Hamilton, New York; parts of his essay are from a book on poetry and politics, to be published by Viking. He is author of *The Survivor: An Anatomy of Life in the Death Camps*. The new collection from San Francisco's **William Dickey** will be *The King of the Golden River*, due soon from Pterodactyl Press. **Blaga Dimitrova** is a Bulgarian poet who went to Vietnam during the war, and returned with a child, whom she raised. *Hard Country* is **Sharon Doubiago**'s epic poem (West End Press); "Ground Zero" was also featured in Empty Bowl's *Dalmo'ma Anthology*, and won a Pushcart Prize in 1984. Doubiago's book of stories, *The Book of Seeing with One's Own Eyes* is coming from Scribner's. **Eugene Dubnov** is a Russian emigré living in London. **Stephen Dunn**'s fifth collection, *Not Dancing*, was published in 1984 by Carnegie-Mellon University Press. He teaches at Stockton State College in New Jersey and at Columbia University. **John Elder** is an English and environmental studies professor at Middlebury College and has recently completed a book entitled *Imagining the Earth: Contemporary Poetry and the Vision of Nature*. **Louise Erdrich** grew up in North Dakota, a member of the Turtle Mountain Band of Chippewa, and now lives in New Hampshire. She has two new books, *Jacklight* (poems) and *Love Medicine* (a novel), both from Holt, Rinehart & Winston. **Patricia Goedicke**'s sixth book of poems, *The Wind of Our Going*, is coming from Copper Canyon Press. She has lived for years in Mexico and now teaches in Montana. Author of *Woman and Nature: The Roaring Inside Her*, *Pornography and Silence*, and *Made from This Earth* (all from Harper & Row), **Susan Griffin** lives in Berkeley; she is working on *The First and the Last: A Woman Thinks About War* and an audio-tape project in collaboration with Honor Moore. Griffin's "Prayer for Continuation" is featured in the 1985 War Resisters League calendar. **Emily Grosholz**'s first book of poems is *The River Painter* (University of Illinois Press). She teaches philosophy at Penn State. **Katharine Haake** is a Ph.D. candidate in English and Creative Writing at the University of Utah. **John Haines** has homesteaded in Alaska for over twenty years and is author of *News from the Glacier: Selected Poems* (Wesleyan University Press) and *Three Days* (Graywolf). Ireland's **Seamus Heaney** teaches part of each year at Harvard. His new book is *Station Island*, to be published by Farrar, Straus and Giroux in 1984. **David Ignatow** has been President of the Poetry Society of America and is author of *Whisper to the Earth* (Atlantic Monthly Press) and *The Notebooks of David Ignatow* (Sheep Meadow Press). **Mark Johnston** teaches rhetoric and composition at Quinnipiac College in Connecticut. **Galway Kinnell**'s *Selected Poems* (Houghton-Mifflin) won the Pulitzer Prize in 1983. **Aaron Kramer** has published two dozen books, including *The Burning Bush: Poems and Other Writings, 1940-1980* (Cornwall Books). Poet and fiction writer **Maxine Kumin** has recently collected two retrospective Viking editions: *Our Ground Time Here Will Be Brief* (poems) and *Why Can't We Live Together Like Civilized Human Beings?* (stories); she lives in New Hampshire. **Eric Larsen** teaches at John Jay College of Criminal Justice in New York and has published essays and stories in *NER/BLQ*, *Prairie Schooner*, *The New Republic*, *Harper's*, and elsewhere. **Sydney Lea** is a founding editor of *New England Review*, and author of three books: *Searching the Drowned Man* and *The Floating Candles* (both poetry, from University of Illinois Press), and *Gothic to Fantastic: Readings in Supernatural Fiction*. **Denise Levertov** is a longtime activist with two recent New Directions collections, *Candles in Babylon* (poems) and *Light Up the Cave* (essays). **Peter Makuck** is editor of *Tar River Poetry* and author of *Breaking and Entering* (stories, University of Illinois Press), and *Where We Live* (poems, BOA Editions). **William Matthews**'s latest book is *A Happy Childhood* (Atlantic-Little, Brown). **Honor Moore** lives in New York City and rural Connecticut. Her verse play *Mourning Pictures* was produced on Broadway in 1974 and is included in *The New Women's Theatre*. She is at work on a biography of her grandmother, the painter Margarett Sargent. "Spuyten Duyvil" has been given a setting by classical guitarist Janet Marlow, and will be available on an audio-tape, also featuring work by Susan Griffin and Margie Adam, from the Watershed Foundation. **Howard Moss** is the poetry editor of *The New Yorker* and has written eleven books of poems and three of criticism; his new book of poems is *Rules of Sleep*, from Atheneum. Poet, playwright, and novelist **Robert Nichols**, a member of the Ompompanoosuc Affinity Group in Thetford, Vermont, has published books with City Lights and Penny Each Press, as well as the landmark utopian tetralogy *Daily Lives in Nghsi-Altai* (New Directions). Knopf published **Sharon Olds**'s *The Dead and the Living* in 1984; her *Satan Says* (University of Pittsburgh Press) won the 1981 San Francisco Poetry Center Award. **Grace Paley**'s *The Little Disturbances of Man* and *Enormous Changes at the Last Minute* have had a major impact on the contemporary short story, and her third collection will appear in the spring of 1985. She has been arrested many times for peaceful obstruction of violence. A member of the Feminary editorial collective, **Minnie Bruce Pratt**'s first book of poems is *The Sound of One Fork* (Night Heron); she now lives in Washington, D.C. **Carolyn Ross** has been making a transition as a writer from poetry to fiction, a change which has coincided with having a child; she and her husband run a bed-and-breakfast inn in Inverness, California. **Jim Schley** was born and raised in Wisconsin, and now lives in New Hampshire where he co-edits *NER/BLQ*; he is a member of a political theater and music group, and a student in the Warren Wilson M.F.A. program. **Kolyo Sevov** is a Bulgarian poet. **Barbara Smith** is a black feminist writer and activist, co-editor of some of the anthologies noted in her essay and a founding member of Kitchen Table: Women of Color Press in Brooklyn, New York. **William Stafford** has worked in beet fields and oil refineries, taught at many universities, and written more than a dozen books of poems including *A Glass Face in the Rain* (Harper & Row), *Smoke's Way* (Graywolf Press), and *Segues: A Correspondence in Poetry* (with Marvin Bell, Godine). **Robert Penn Warren** has been three times a winner of the Pulitzer Prize, and continues to write poetry, fiction, and criticism. **William Zaranka** lives in Denver, and has published *The Brand-X Anthologies of Fiction and Poetry* (Applewood) and *A Mirror Driven Through Nature*; the Blessing character in his sequence-in-progress is a military satellite engineer who spies on the Russians and Chinese, but also on his own bald spot and deteriorating marriage.